Benson John Lossing, William Barritt

Pictorial History of the Civil War in the United States of America

Benson John Lossing, William Barritt

Pictorial History of the Civil War in the United States of America

ISBN/EAN: 9783337404666

Printed in Europe, USA, Canada, Australia, Japan

Cover: Foto ©ninafisch / pixelio.de

More available books at **www.hansebooks.com**

PICTORIAL HISTORY

OF

THE CIVIL WAR

IN THE

UNITED STATES OF AMERICA.

By BENSON J. LOSSING.

ILLUSTRATED BY MANY HUNDRED ENGRAVINGS ON WOOD, BY LOSSING AND
BARRITT, FROM SKETCHES BY THE AUTHOR AND OTHERS.

VOLUME I.

HARTFORD:
THOMAS BELKNAP, PUBLISHER,

PREFACE.

HE task of making a record of the events of the late Civil War in our Republic is not a pleasant one for an American citizen. It would be more consonant with his wishes to bury in oblivion all knowledge of those events which compose the materials of the sorrowful story of a strife among his brethren, of terrible energy and woeful operations. But that privilege is denied him. The din of the conflict was heard all over the world, and people of all nations were spectators of the scene. The fact cannot be hidden. It has become a part of the history of the inhabitants of the earth, and will forever occupy a conspicuous place in the annals of mankind. What remains for the American citizen to do, is to see that the *stylus* of history shall make a truthful record.

I imposed upon myself the task of making, so far as my ability and an honest purpose would permit, a correct delineation of the events of the conflict, carefully drawn by the pen and pencil, for the consideration and advantage of posterity. I entitle my work "A History of the Civil War," but I ask for it no higher consideration than that of a faithful CHRONICLE, having the form of history, and aspiring to perform its highest duty, namely : to inspire mankind with a love of justice and a hatred of its opposite, and of every thing that impedes the onward and upward march of humanity.

Taking it for granted that the reader, with the facts plainly set before him, is capable of forming just conclusions, I have confined my labors chiefly to the recording of those facts ; and have only given opinions and speculations concerning their relations, and the evident motives of the chief actors in the drama, sufficient for hints for thought and premises for reasoning, without enlarging into argument or endeavoring to forestall the judgment. For the assistance of that judgment, there will be found in the concluding chapter of this work an outline history of the settlement of our country ; of the growth of the nation ; of the system of slave-labor, and its influence upon society ; of the cotton-plant, and its relations and power ; of immigration from Europe, and its results; and of the alienation of feeling produced by controversies on the subject of slavery. These are elements of the great Cause, of which the civil war was the Effect.

Satisfied that the Rebellion was the work of a few ambitious men, who for selfish purposes, and without excuse, conspired to overthrow the Republic, I have given prominence to their sayings and those of their co-workers and abettors, not with a partisan spirit, to keep animosities alive (for I would gladly blot their utterances from the memory of man), but that posterity may know, and profit by the knowledge, how and by whom the people of a group of States were deceived, and cruelly wronged, and arrayed against their government, which has been seldom accused, and never convicted, of a single act of injustice or oppression.[1] It seemed just to the loyal people of the land everywhere to make this record, and in their name to disclaim these utterances as being any indication of the spirit and temper of the American people.

The Republic has survived the strife within its bosom, and it now bears on, in the great procession of nations, its precious burden of Free Institutions and Democratic Ideas, as nobly and vigorously as ever. The Union has been preserved, and its broad mantle of Love and Charity covers all its children with its ample folds. There should be no more strife—no more alienations ; for the true interest of each individual of the family is the highest interest of all. If the sorrowful Past may not be forgotten (and it is best that it should not be forgotten), let the remembrance of it be a chastening monitor and tutor ; and let all who feel aggrieved be willing to forgive.

Wishing to secure the advantages of a personal knowledge, by actual examination, of the principal battle-fields of the war, and the topography of the regions over which the great armies moved, and to make sketches of whatever might seem useful as illustrations of the subject, I did not begin the preparation of this work for the

---

[1] See speech of Alexander H. Stephens at Milledgeville, Georgia, November 14, 1860, noticed on pages 53 to 57, inclusive, of this volume.

press until the close of the conflict, late in the spring of 1865. Then the proportions of that conflict were known, and its several events were so well comprehended, that it was not a difficult task to give to each act and scene its relative position and due prominence, while compressing the whole narrative into a space so small as to make the chronicle accessible to the great body of my countrymen. I have endeavored to give a popular narrative of the struggle without much criticism, and as free from technical terms and tediousness of detail as possible, leaving the preparation of a scientific and critical history of the war to military experts, who are more competent for the task.

I gladly availed myself of the labors of others with pen and pencil, who kindly permitted me to make use of unpublished materials—such as drawings, photographs, diaries, and letters ; and I am specially indebted to the courtesy of the proprietors of *Harper's Weekly* and *Frank Leslie's Illustrated Newspaper*, whose artists accompanied the great armies throughout the whole struggle, and preserved the lineaments of a thousand objects which were soon swept away by the storms of war. I was accorded free access to all official reports allowed to be made public ; and chiefly from these and the drawings of engineers, the narratives of marches, battles, and sieges were compiled, with accompanying maps and plans. In the work will be found the portraits of the prominent actors, civil and military, of both parties to the conflict ; also views and plans of battle-grounds ; head-quarters of officers ; weapons and ships of war ; forts ; arsenals ; medals of honor, and other gifts of gratitude ; costumes of soldiers ; flags ; banners ; badges ; and a great variety of other objects whereby the eye may be instructed concerning the materials used in the conflict.

The engravings, whilst they embellish the book, have been introduced for the higher purposes of instruction, and are confined to the service of illustrating facts. They have been prepared under my direct supervision ; and great pains have been taken to make them correct delineations of the objects sought to be represented. In each volume will be found a table of contents, and a list of illustrations ; and, at the close of the work, a copious analytical index. There will also be found biographical sketches of the prominent actors in the war, civil and military, arranged in cyclopedia form, and making an important Biographical Dictionary.

I am profoundly grateful to my personal friends, and to my

countrymen of every degree, from the most humble citizen and sol-
dier to statesmen, army and navy officers of every rank, governors,
and the President and his cabinet ministers, who kindly aided me
in my labors in the collection of materials for this work.   It would
be a pleasant privilege to mention the name of each, but they are
legion, and for obvious reasons it may not be done.

B. J. L.

THE RIDGE, DOVER PLAINS, N. Y.

VOLUME I.

CHAPTER I.

POLITICAL CONVENTIONS IN 1860.

CHAPTER II.

PRELIMINARY REBELLIOUS MOVEMENTS.

CHAPTER III.

ASSEMBLING OF CONGRESS.—THE PRESIDENT'S MESSAGE.

CHAPTER IV.

SEDITIOUS MOVEMENTS IN CONGRESS.—SECESSION IN SOUTH CAROLINA, AND ITS EFFECTS.

CHAPTER V.

EVENTS IN CHARLESTON AND CHARLESTON HARBOR IN DECEMBER, 1860.—THE CONSPIRATORS ENCOURAGED BY THE GOVERNMENT POLICY.

CHAPTER VI.

AFFAIRS AT THE NATIONAL CAPITAL.—WAR COMMENCED IN CHARLESTON HARBOR.

CHAPTER VII.

SECESSION CONVENTIONS IN SIX STATES.

CHAPTER VIII.

ATTITUDE OF THE BORDER SLAVE-LABOR STATES, AND OF THE FREE-LABOR STATES.

CHAPTER IX.

PROCEEDINGS IN CONGRESS.—DEPARTURE OF CONSPIRATORS.

CHAPTER X.

PEACE MOVEMENTS.—CONVENTION OF CONSPIRATORS AT MONTGOMERY.

CHAPTER XI.

THE MONTGOMERY CONVENTION.—TREASON OF GENERAL TWIGGS.—LINCOLN AND BUCHANAN AT THE CAPITAL.

CHAPTER XII.

THE INAUGURATION OF PRESIDENT LINCOLN, AND THE IDEAS AND POLICY OF THE GOVERNMENT.

CHAPTER XIII.

THE SIEGE AND EVACUATION OF FORT SUMTER.

CHAPTER XIV.

THE GREAT UPRISING OF THE PEOPLE.

CHAPTER XV.

SIEGE OF FORT PICKENS.—DECLARATION OF WAR.—THE VIRGINIA CONSPIRATORS, AND THE PROPOSED CAPTURE OF WASHINGTON CITY.

CHAPTER XVI.

SECESSION OF VIRGINIA AND NORTH CAROLINA DECLARED.—SEIZURE OF HARPER'S FERRY AND GOSPORT NAVY YARD.—THE FIRST TROOPS IN WASHINGTON FOR ITS DEFENSE.

CHAPTER XVII.

EVENTS IN AND NEAR THE NATIONAL CAPITAL.

CHAPTER XVIII.

THE CAPITAL SECURED.—MARYLAND SECESSIONISTS SUBDUED.—CONTRIBUTIONS BY THE PEOPLE.

CHAPTER XIX.

EVENTS IN THE MISSISSIPPI VALLEY.—THE INDIANS.

CHAPTER XX.

COMMENCEMENT OF CIVIL WAR.

CHAPTER XXI.

BEGINNING OF THE WAR IN SOUTHEASTERN VIRGINIA.

CHAPTER XXII.

THE WAR ON THE POTOMAC AND IN WESTERN VIRGINIA.

CHAPTER XXIII.

THE WAR IN MISSOURI.—DOINGS OF THE CONFEDERATE "CONGRESS,"—AFFAIRS IN BALTIMORE.—PIRACIES.

CHAPTER XXIV.

THE CALLED SESSION OF CONGRESS.—FOREIGN RELATIONS.—BENEVOLENT ORGANIZATIONS.—THE OPPOSING ARMIES.

CHAPTER XXV.

BATTLE OF BULL'S RUN.

VOLUME I.

THE CIVIL WAR.

CHAPTER I.

THE POLITICAL CONVENTIONS IN 1860.

IN the spring of the year 1861, a civil war was kindled in the United States of America, which has neither a pattern in character nor a precedent in causes recorded in the history of mankind. It appears in the annals of the race as a mighty phenomenon, but not an inexplicable one. Gazers upon it at this moment,* when its awfully grand and mysterious proportions rather fill the mind with wonder than excite the reason, look for the half-hidden springs of its existence in different directions among the obscurities of theory. There is a general agreement, however, that the terrible war was clearly the fruit of a conspiracy against the nationality of the Republic, and an attempt, in defiance of the laws of Divine Equity, to establish an Empire upon a basis of injustice and a denial of the dearest rights of man. That conspiracy budded when the Constitution of the Republic became the supreme law of the land,¹ and, under the culture of disloyal and ambitious men, after gradual development and long ripening, assumed the form and substance of a rebellion of a few arrogant land and

* 1862.

---

¹ Immediately after the adoption of the National Constitution, and the beginning of the National career, in 1789, the family and State pride of Virginians could not feel contented in a sphere of equality in which that Constitution placed all the States. It still claimed for that Commonwealth a superiority, and a right to political and social domination in the Republic. Disunion was openly and widely talked of in Virginia, as a necessary conservator of State supremacy, during Washington's first term as President of the United States, and became more and more a concrete political dogma. It was because of the prevalence of this dangerous and unpatriotic sentiment in his native State, which was spreading in the Slave-labor States, that Washington gave to his countrymen that magnificent plea for Union—his Farewell Address. According to John Randolph of Roanoke, "the Grand Arsenal of Richmond, Virginia, was built with an eye to putting down the Administration of Mr. Adams (the immediate successor of Washington in the office of President) *with the bayonet*, if it could not be accomplished by other means."—*Speech of Randolph in the House of Representatives*, January, 1817.

2

slave holders against popular government. It was the rebellion of an OLI-GARCHY against the PEOPLE, with whom the sovereign power is rightfully lodged.

We will not here discuss the subject of the remote and half-hidden springs of the rebellion, which so suddenly took on the hideous dignity of a great civil war. We will deal simply with palpable facts, and leave the disquisition of theories until we shall have those facts arranged in proper order and relations. Then we may, far better than now, comprehend the soul of the great historic phenomenon that so startled the nations, and com-manded the profound attention of the civilized world.

With the choice of Presidential Electors, in the autumn of 1860, the open career of the living conspirators against American Nationality com-menced; and with the nominations of the candidates for the office of Chief Magistrate of the Republic, in the spring and early summer of that year, we will begin our HISTORY OF THE CIVIL WAR.

VIEW OF THE CITY OF CHARLESTON, IN 1860.

The two chief political parties into which the voters of the country were divided in 1860, were called, respectively, *Democratic* and *Republican*. These titles really had no intrinsic significance, as indices of principles, when applied to either organization, but were used by the leaders as ensigns are used in war, namely, as rallying-points for the contending hosts—familiar in form if not intelligible in character. That year Presidential electors were to be chosen; and, in accordance with a long-established custom, represen-tatives were appointed by the people, to meet in conventions and choose the candidates.

The Democratic party moved first. Its representatives were summoned to assemble in Charleston, a pleasant city of forty thousand inhabitants, and a considerable commercial mart. It is spread over the point of a low sandy cape, at the confluence of the waters of the Ashley and Cooper

Rivers, on the seacoast of South Carolina, and far away from the centers of population and the great forces of the Republic.

The delegates, almost six hundred in number, and representing thirty-two States, assembled on the 23d of April * in the great hall of the South Carolina Institute,[1] on Meeting Street, in which three thousand persons might be comfortably seated. The doors were opened at noon. The day was very warm. A refreshing shower had laid the dust at eleven o'clock, and purified the air.

* 1860.

The delegates rapidly assembled. Favored spectators of both sexes soon filled the galleries. The buzz of conversation was silenced by the voice of Judge David A. Smalley, of Vermont, the Chairman of the National Democratic Committee, who called the Convention to order. Francis B. Flournoy, a citizen of the State of Arkansas, was chosen temporary chairman.—

THE SOUTH CAROLINA INSTITUTE.

He took his seat without making a speech, when the Rev. Charles Hanckel, of Charleston, read a prayer, and the Convention proceeded to business.

The session of the first day was occupied in the work of organization. It was evident, from the first hour, that the spirit of the Slave system, which had become the very Nemesis of the nation, was there, full fraught with mischievous intent. It was a spirit potential as Ariel in the creation of elemental strife. For several months, premonitions of a storm, that threatened danger to the integrity of the organization there represented, had been abundant. Violently discordant elements were now in close contact. The clouds rapidly thickened, and before the sun went down on that first day of the session, all felt that a fierce tempest was impending, which might topple from its foundations, laid by Jefferson, the venerable political fabric known as the Democratic Party, which he and his friends had reared sixty years before.

On the morning of the second day of the session, Caleb Cushing, of Massachusetts, was chosen permanent President of the Convention, and a vice-president and secretary for each State were appointed. The choice of President was very satisfactory. Mr. Cushing was a man of much experience in politics and legislation. He was possessed of wide intellectual culture, and was a sagacious observer of men. He was then sixty years of

---

1 This building, in which the famous South Carolina Ordinance of Secession was *signed* (it was *adopted* in St. Andrew's Hall), late in December, 1860, was destroyed by fire in December, 1861. St. Andrew's Hall, in which the conspirators against the Republic who seceded from the Democratic Convention now under consideration assembled, and in which the South Carolina Ordinance of Secession was adopted by the unanimous voice of a Convention, was destroyed at the same time. Everything about the site of these buildings, made infamous in history because of the wicked acts performed in them, yet (1865) exhibits a ghastly picture of desolation.

age; his features expressed great mental and moral energy, and his voice was clear and musical.

On taking the chair, Mr. Cushing addressed the Convention with great vigor. He declared it to be the mission of the Democratic party to "reconcile popular freedom with constituted order," and to maintain "the sacred reserved rights of the Sovereign States."

He declared the Republicans to be those who were "laboring to overthrow the Constitution," and "aiming to produce in this country a permanent sectional conspiracy— a traitorous sectional conspiracy of one half of the States of the Union against the other half; those who, impelled by the stupid and half insane spirit of faction and fanaticism, would hurry our land on to revolution and to civil war." He declared it to be the "high and noble part of the Democratic party of the Union to withstand—to strike down and conquer" these "banded enemies of the Constitution."[1] These utterances formed a key-note that harmonized with the feelings of a large body of the delegates, and was a symphony to their action.

CALEB CUSHING.

At the close of the second day the Convention was in fair working order. Some contests for seats were undecided, there being two sets of delegates from New York and Illinois; but the vitally important *Committee on Resolutions*, composed of one delegate from each State, had been appointed without much delay. It was the business of that committee to perform the difficult and delicate task of making a platform of principles for the action of the Convention, and the stand-point of the party during the approaching canvass and election. For this purpose it had been sent to Masonic Hall, at five o'clock in the afternoon; and then and there the electric spark, which kindled the prepared combustibles of civil war into a quick and devouring flame, was elicited by the attrition of radically opposing ideas.

The subject of Slavery, as we have observed, was the troubling spirit of the Convention. It appeared in the open Hall, and it was specially apparent in the room of the Committee on Resolutions. A large number of the delegates from the Slave-labor States had come instructed, and were resolved, to demand from the Convention a candidate and a platform which should promise a guaranty for the speedy and practical recognition, by the General Government and the people, of the system of Slavery as a national and permanent institution. Impelled by this resolution, they had determined to prevent the nomination of Stephen A. Douglas of Illinois (an able statesman, and effective popular orator, then in the full vigor of middle age), who was the most prominent candidate for the suffrages of the Convention. They opposed him because he was so committed to the doctrine of "Popular Sovereignty," as it was called,—that is to say, the doctrine of the right of the people of any Territory of the Republic to decide whether Slavery should

[1] *Official Proceedings of the Democratic National Convention, held in 1860, at Charleston and Baltimore,* page 17.

or should not exist within its borders,—that he could not, with honor or consistency, make any further concessions to the Slave interest. This, an' the positive committal of the Democratic party to a pro-slavery policy in the administration of the National Government, were the chief business of several delegates in the Convention who were led by such men as John Slidell, of Louisiana, and William L. Yancey, of Alabama, then, and long before, arch-conspirators against the life of the Republic.

In June, 1856, a National Democratic Convention was held at Cincinnati, when James Buchanan was nominated for President of the United States. A platform was then framed, composed of many resolutions and involved declarations of principles, drawn by the hand of Benjamin F. Hallet, of Boston. These embodied the substance of resolutions on the subject of Slavery, drawn up by Benjamin F. Butler, of Massachusetts (afterwards a major-general in the armies of the Republic), and adopted by the Democratic Convention of that State. On the topic of Slavery and State supremacy, the resolutions were clear and explicit. They recognized the doctrine of Popular Sovereignty as " embodying the only sound and safe solution of the Slavery question, upon which the great national idea of the people of this whole country can repose in its determined conservation of the Union, and non-interference of Congress with Slavery in the Territories or in the District of Columbia." This doctrine harmonized with the spirit of popular government; and the platform, of which it was an essential part, was accepted by the Democratic party throughout the Union, as a true exposition of their principles and policy. With this understanding, Mr. Butler, now a member of the Committee on Resolutions sitting in Masonic Hall, on that warm April evening in 1860, proposed as a platform for the Convention and the party the one constructed at Cincinnati four years before, without addition or alteration. He offered a resolution to that effect, when, to the surprise of the representatives of the Free-labor States, the proposition was rejected by a vote of seventeen States (only two of them free) against fifteen States. Recently created Oregon gave the casting vote against it, and, with California, was arrayed on the side of the Slave-labor States.

The majority now proposed an affirmance of the Cincinnati platform, but with additional resolutions, the most vital of which declared that Congress had no power to abolish Slavery in the Territories, and that Territorial Legislatures had no power to abolish Slavery in any Territory, nor to prohibit the introduction of Slavery therein, nor to exclude Slavery therefrom, or to impair or destroy the right of property in slaves by any legislation whatever. This resolution was a positive rejection of the doctrine of Popular Sovereignty. The minority of the committee, composed wholly of delegates from the Free-labor States, and representing a majority of the Presidential electors (one hundred and seventy-two against one hundred and twenty-seven), were amazed because of the bad faith and arrogant assumptions of their Southern brethren. It was clearly seen that the latter were united, evidently by preconcert, in a determination to demand from the people of the Free-labor States further and most offensive concessions to their greed for political domination.

The manhood of the minority was evoked, and they resolved that the limit of concession was reached, and that they would yield to no further demands. They at once proposed an affirmance of the Cincinnati platform in letter and spirit, at the same time expressing, by resolution, a willingness to abide by any decision of the Supreme Court of the United States on questions of constitutional law. They offered a word for conciliation by denouncing, in another resolution, the acts of certain State Legislatures known as "Personal Liberty Laws, as "hostile in character, subversive of the Constitution, and revolutionary in their effects." Mr. Butler was opposed to making even this concession, and adhered to his proposition for a simple affirmance of the Cincinnati platform.

The labors of the Committee resulted, on the evening of the fourth day of the session, in the production of three reports, and on the following morning these were submitted to the Convention: the majority report by William W. Avery, of North Carolina; the minority report, drawn by H. B. Payne, of Ohio, and a resolution for the affirmance of the Cincinnati platform without alteration, by B. F. Butler.

Mr. Avery opened debate on the subject, by frankly assuring the Convention that if the doctrine of Popular Sovereignty should be adopted as the doctrine of the Democratic party, the members of the Convention from the Slave-labor States, and their constituents, would consider it as dangerous and subversive of their rights, as the adoption of the principle of Congressional interference or prohibition. From that time until Monday, the 30th of April,ᵃ the debate was continued, in the midst of much   ᵃ 1860. confusion and disorder in the Convention. The streets of Charleston in the pleasant evenings resounded with music, the speeches of politicians, and the huzzas of the multitude. Society there was in a bubble of excitement, and the final vote of the Convention on the resolutions was awaited with the most lively interest. The hour for that decision at length arrived.   ᵇ April, It was on the morning of the 30th.ᵇ The Hall was densely   1860. crowded. A vote was first taken on Butler's resolution. It was rejected by a decisive majority. The minority report—the Douglas platform—which had been slightly modified, was now offered by B. M. Samuels, of Iowa. It was adopted by a handsome majority. In the Convention now, as in the Committee, the voices of Oregon and California, Free-labor States, were with those of the Slave-labor States.

Preconcerted rebellion now lifted its head defiantly. The spirit manifested in the resolutions, speeches, and deportment of the representatives of the Slave interest, now assumed tangible form, in action. L. P. Walker, who was afterward one of the most active insurgents against the National Government, as the so-called Secretary of War of Jefferson Davis, led the way. He spoke for the delegates from Alabama, who had been instructed by the convention that appointed them not to acquiesce in or submit to any Popular Sovereignty platform, and, in the event of such being adopted, to withdraw from the Convention. That contingency had now occurred, and the Alabama delegates formally withdrew, in accordance with a previous arrangement. They were followed by all the delegates from Mississippi, all but two from Louisiana, all from Florida and Texas, three from Arkansas, and all from South Carolina. On the following morning, twenty-six of the thirty-four Georgia delegates withdrew; and Senator Bayard and Representative Whiteley, delegates from Delaware, also left the Convention and joined the seceders, who had repaired to St. Andrew's Hall the previous evening for consultation.

The disruption of the Democratic party represented in Convention was now complete. The wedge of Slavery had split it beyond restoration. The event had been amply provided for in secret; and when D. C. Glenn, of Mississippi, in announcing the withdrawal of the delegates from that State, said, " I tell Southern men here, and, for them, I tell the North, that in less than sixty days you will find a united South standing side by side with us," there was long and vehement cheering, especially from the South Carolinians, who were joyous over the result. Charleston, that night, was the scene of unbounded pleasurable excitement.

So the arrogant representatives of the Slave interest, in contempt of the democratic principle of acquiescence in the fairly expressed will of the majority, which lies at the foundation of all order in popular government, and with an eye single to the accomplishment of an intensely selfish end, began a rebellion, first against the dominant party then in possession of the National Government, and secondly against that Government itself, which resulted in a bloody civil war, and the utter destruction of the vast and cherished interest, for the conservation of which they cast down the gauntlet defiantly and invited the arbitrament of the sword.

At twilight, on the eighth day of the session of the Convention,* when the excitement occasioned by the withdrawal of many delegates had somewhat subsided, that body proceeded to ballot for a candidate for the Presidency of the Republic. At least two hundred votes were necessary to a choice. Stephen A. Douglas led off with at least fifty less than the requisite number. There was very little variation as the voting *May, 1860.

went on. Finally, on the tenth day, when fifty-seven ballotings had been taken with no prospect of a change, it was agreed to adjourn the Convention, to meet in the city of Baltimore, in Maryland, on the eighteenth day of June following. It was also resolved to invite the Democracy of the several States to make provision for supplying all vacancies in their respective delegations to the Convention when it should reassemble.

The seceding delegates partially organized a convention at St. Andrew's Hall, on the evening after their withdrawal from the regular body. On the following day, at

ST. ANDREW'S HALL.[1]

noon, they assembled at Military Hall, when they chose James A. Bayard, of Delaware, to be their president. They declared themselves, by resolution offered by Mr. Yancey, to be entitled to the style of the

---

[1] In this building, as we have observed, the Secession Convention of South Carolina politicians was assembled when it passed the Ordinance of Secession, on the 20th of December, 1860.

" Constitutional Convention," and sneeringly called those whom they had abandoned, the " Rump Convention." On the second day of their session they met in the Theater.[1] The dress circle was crowded with the women of Charleston. They had hitherto filled the galleries of the Institute Hall. Their sympathies were with the seceders, and they now followed them.

President Bayard, a dignified, courtly gentleman, sat near the foot-lights of the stage. The painted scene behind him was that of the Borgia Palace,[2] around which clustered associations of great crimes. The actors on this occasion, contrary to precedent, occupied the pit, or parquette; and there they performed only the first act of a drama to which the whole civilized world became amazed spectators. They adopted the report of the majority, offered by Mr. Avery in the regular Convention, as their platform of principles, but went no further then. They refrained from nominating a candidate for the Presidency of the Republic, and refused to listen to a proposition to send forth an address to the people. Their appointed work for the present was finished. They had accomplished the positive disruption of the Democratic party, which, as a Southern historian of the war says, had become " demoralized" on " the Slavery question," and were " unreliable and rotten,"[3] because they held independent views on that great topic of national discussion. The paralysis or destruction of that party would give the Presidency to a Republican candidate, and then the conspirators would have a wished-for pretext for rebellion.[4] The seceders were confident that their work had been effectually performed, and their desired object attained. They well knew that their class held such absolute political control in the Slave-labor States, that the great mass of their constituency would applaud their action and follow their lead. Reposing upon this knowledge, they could afford to wait for further developments; so, on the evening of the 3d of May,[a] they adjourned to meet in the city of Richmond, in * 1860. Virginia, on the second Monday of June following, for further action. To that Convention they invited the Democracy of the country who might sympathize with their movement and their platform to send representatives.

The seceders reassembled in Metropolitan Hall (on Franklin Street, near Governor), in Richmond, at the appointed time, namely, on Monday, the 11th day of June. In the mean time some of the leading Southern Congressmen, among whom were Robert Toombs, of Georgia, and other conspirators, had issued an address from Washington City, urging that the Richmond Convention should refrain from all important action, and adjourn to Baltimore, and there, re-entering the regular Convention, if possible defeat the nomination of Mr. Douglas, and thus, as they said, with well-feigned honesty of expression, " make a final effort to preserve the harmony and unity of the Democratic party." The consequence was, that the Convention at Richmond

---

[1] This was the fourth place in which the conspirators met in the course of forty-eight hours. All of these public buildings are now (1865) in ruins.

[2] History of the National Political Conventions in 1860; by M. Halstead, an Eye-witness, page 100.

[3] First Year of the War; by Edward A. Pollard, Richmond, 1862, page 28.

[4] When, in 1832 and 1833, Calhoun and his associates in South Carolina attempted to strike a deadly blow at our nationality, they made a protective tariff, which they called an oppression of the cotton-growing States, the pretext. In May, 1833, President Jackson, in a letter to the Rev. A. J. Crawford, of Georgia, after speaking of the trouble he had endured on account of the Nullifiers, said, " The Tariff was only the pretext, and Disunion and a Southern Confederacy the real object. The next pretext will be the Negro or Slavery question."

was respectable in talent, but small in numbers, and wicked in conception and design.

On motion of a son of John C. Calhoun, who was chairman of the Com-

mittee on Organization, John Irwin, of Alabama, was chosen president of the Convention. It then proceeded to action, under a little embarrassment at first. There were delegates from the city of New York begging for admission to seats.[1] They were finally treated with courteous contempt, by being simply admitted to the floor of the Convention as tolerated "commissioners," and were regarded by some as spies. In this matter, as in others, the proceedings were cautiously

METROPOLITAN HALL.[2]

managed. The leaders allowed no definite action. An expression of opinion concerning the platforms offered at Charleston was suppressed; and on the second day of the session, while a "Colonel Baldwin," of the New York "commissioners," smarting under the lash of W. L. Barry, of Mississippi, who charged him with "abusing the courtesy of the Convention" by talking of the "horrors of disunion," was asking forgiveness in an abject manner,[3] the Convention adjourned, to meet at the same place on the 21st of the month.[4] Most of the delegates then hastened to Baltimore, pursuant to the plan of the Congressional conspirators, while the South   * June, 1860. Carolina delegation, who assumed to be special managers of the treasonable drama, remained in Richmond, awaiting further developments of the plot.

The adjourned Democratic National Convention reassembled in the Front Street Theater, on Front Street, opposite Low Street, in Baltimore, on Monday, the 18th day of June. The parquette and stage were occupied by the delegates, and the dress circle was filled by spectators—a large portion of whom were women. The delicate and difficult question concerning the admission to seats in the Convention of representatives of States whose delegates had withdrawn from that body, was the first to present it-

---

[1] These delegates appear to have been representatives of an association of some kind in the city of New York, who sympathized with the Secessionists. They exhibited, as credentials, a certificate of the " Trustees of the National Democratic Hall " in New York, signed by "Samuel B. Williams, *Chairman*, M. Dudley Bean, Secretary of the Trustees." It was also signed by William Beach Lawrence, *Chairman*, and James B. Bensel, *Secretary*, of an Executive Committee; and Thaddeus P. Mott, *Chairman*, and J. Lawrence, *Secretary* of the Association, whatever it was. These certified that Gideon J. Tucker and Dr. Charles Edward Lewis Stuart had been appointed "delegates at large from the Association;" and that Colonel Baldwin, Isaac Lawrence, James B. Bensel, and James Villiers, had been appointed *Delegates*, and N. Drake Parsons, James S. Selby, M. Dudley Bean, and A. W. Gilbert, *Alternatives*, "to represent the Association at the Richmond Convention, for the nomination of President and Vice-president," &c.

[2] This building was formerly occupied as a Presbyterian Church, and known as that of Dr. Plummer's.

[3] Halstead's *History of the National Political Conventions in 1860*, page 156.

self. Mr. Cushing, again in the chair, refused to make any decision, and referred the whole matter to the Convention. It was claimed, that the seceding delegates had a right to re-enter the Convention if they chose to do so. This right was denied, and the language of the resolution respecting the adjournment at Charleston, by which the States represented by the seceders were called upon to "fill vacancies," was referred to as an expression of the Convention, if fairly interpreted, against the right of the seceders to return.

It was proposed, also, that no delegate should be admitted to a seat, unless he would pledge himself to abide by the action of a majority of the Convention, and support its nominations. Debate speedily ensued. It was hot and acrimonious during, at least, six hours on that first day of the session; and in the evening there were two mass meetings of the Democracy in the streets of Baltimore, at which vehement speeches were heard for three hours, by tens of thousands of people, citizens and strangers.

FRONT STREET THEATER, IN BALTIMORE, IN 1860.

On the following morning, the subject of contesting delegations was referred to the committee on credentials. They could not agree; and on the fourth day of the session* two reports were submitted, the majority report recommending the admission of Douglas delegates (in place of seceders) from Louisiana and Alabama, and parts of the delegations from other States. The minority report was against the admission of the new delegates. These reports were discussed with great warmth, which sometimes reached the point of fierce personal quarrels. The pro-slavery men gave free scope to the expression of their opinions and feelings; and one of them, a mercantile dealer in slaves, from Georgia, named Gaulden, advocated the reopening of the Slave-trade, and thought he should live to see the day when the doctrines which he advocated would be "the doctrines of Massachusetts and of the North." He spoke in language shocking to every right-minded man; yet, while he disgusted a great majority of his hearers, he elicited the applause of many.

* June 21, 1860.

Finally, on Friday, the 22d, the majority report was adopted, and the places of most of the seceders were filled by Douglas men. Again there was rebellion against the fairly expressed will of the majority. The whole or a part of the delegations from Virginia, North Carolina, Tennessee, Maryland, California, Delaware, and Missouri, withdrew. That night was a gloomy one for those who earnestly desired the unity of the Democratic party. On the following morning, their hopes were utterly blasted when Mr. Cushing, the President of the Convention, and a majority of the Massachusetts delegation, also withdrew. "We put our withdrawal before you," said Mr. Butler, of that delegation, "upon the simple ground, among others, that there has been a withdrawal, in part, of a majority of the States, and, further (and that, perhaps, more personal to myself), upon the ground that

I will not sit in a Convention where the African Slave-trade—which is piracy by the laws of my country—is approvingly advocated."

On the retirement of Mr. Cushing, Governor David Tod, of Ohio, one of the vice-presidents, took the chair, and the Convention proceeded to ballot for a Presidential candidate. A considerable number of Southern delegates, who were satisfied with the Cincinnati platform, remained in the Convention, and, as their respective States were called, some of them made brief speeches. One of these was Mr. Flournoy, of Arkansas, the temporary Chairman of the Convention at Charleston. "I am a Southern man," he said, "born and reared amid the institution of Slavery. I first learned to whirl the top and bounce the ball with the young African. Everything I own on earth is the result of slave-labor. The bread that feeds my wife and little ones is produced by the labor of slaves. They live on my plantation with every feeling of kindness, as between master and slave. Sir, if I could see that there is anything intended in our platform unfriendly to the institution of Slavery—if I could see that we did not get every constitutional right we are entitled to, I would be the last on earth to submit in this Union; I would myself apply the torch to the magazine, and blow it into atoms, before I would submit to wrong. But I feel that in the doctrines of non-intervention and popular sovereignty is enough to protect the interests of the South."

This speech had a powerful effect upon delegates from the Free-labor States, in favor of Mr. Douglas; and of one hundred and ninety-four and a half votes cast, on the second ballot, he received one hundred and eighty-one and a half, when he was declared duly nominated for the Presidency.

James Fitzpatrick, of Alabama, was nominated for Vice-president. Two days afterward, Fitzpatrick declined the nomination, when the National Committee substituted Herschel V. Johnson, of Georgia.[1] On the evening of the 23d, the Convention made a final adjournment.

The seceders, new and old, assembled at noon on Saturday, the 23d, in the Maryland Institute Hall, situate on Baltimore Street and Marsh Market Space, a room more than three hundred feet in length

THE MARYLAND INSTITUTE IN 1860.

and seventy in breadth, with a gallery extending entirely around. It was capable of seating five thousand people; and it was almost full when the Convention was permanently organized by the appointment of Mr. Cushing to preside. That gentleman was greeted, when he ascended the platform,

---

[1] The National Committee assembled at the National Hotel, in Washington City, on the 25th of June. In it all the States were represented, excepting Delaware, South Carolina, Mississippi, and Oregon.

with the most vociferous applause, and other demonstrations of satisfaction. On taking the chair, he declared that the body then assembled formed the true *National Democratic Convention*, composed, as it was, of delegates duly accredited thereto from more than twenty States. The Convention then proceeded to business with the greatest harmony. They resolved, that the delegates to the Richmond Convention should be requested to unite with their brethren of the *National Democratic Convention*, then assembled, on the same platform of principles with themselves, if they felt authorized to do so. They took seats accordingly. Mr. Avery, of North Carolina, offered the majority report, which he had submitted in Convention at Charleston, and it was adopted without dissent, as the platform of principles of the sitting Convention, and of the party it represented.

After some further business, the Convention proceeded to the nomination of candidates for the Presidency and Vice-presidency, when George B. Loring, of Massachusetts, arose and said : " We have seen the statesmen of Mississippi coming into our own borders and fearlessly defending their principles, ay, and bringing the sectionalism of the North at their feet by their gallantry.[1] We have admiration for this courage, and I trust to live by it and be governed by it. Among all these men to whom we have been led to listen, and whom we admire and respect, there is one standing pre-eminently before this country—a young and gallant son of the South." He then named John C. Breckinridge, of Kentucky, as a nominee for the Presidency.[2] Vehement applause followed. A vote by States was taken, and Breckinridge received eighty-one ballots against twenty-four for Daniel S. Dickinson, of New York. The latter candidate was withdrawn, and the nomination of Breckinridge was declared. Joseph Lane, of Oregon, was nominated for the Vice-presidency; and after a session of only a few hours, the business was ended and the Convention adjourned.[*]

* June 23, 1860.

The South Carolina delegation, who remained in Richmond, formally assembled at Metropolitan Hall on the 21st, according to appointment, and adjourned from day to day until the evening of the 26th, when Mr. Yancey and many others arrived from Baltimore. The Convention then organized for business, which was soon dispatched. The platform and candidates offered to the party by the seceders' Convention at Baltimore were adopted by unanimous vote, with great cheering by the delegates and the crowd who filled the galleries. Then the Convention adjourned.

So ended the Conventions of the divided Democratic party, in the early

---

[1] One of these was Jefferson Davis. In a speech in Faneuil Hall, on the 11th of October, 1858, while denouncing the Abolitionists as disunionists, he said, pointing to the portraits of the elder Adams and others, on the walls:—" If those voices, which breathed the first instincts into the Colony of Massachusetts, and into the other colonies of the United States, to proclaim community—independence—and to assert it against the powerful mother country ; if those voices live here still, how must they feel who come here to preach treason to the Constitution, and assail the Union it ordained and established ? It would seem that their criminal hearts would fear that those voices, so long slumbering, would break their silence ; that those forms which look down from these walls, behind and around, would come forth, to drive from this sacred temple these fanatical men—who deserve it more than did the changers of money and those who sold doves in the temple of the living God." At that very time, that bold, bad man was doubtless plotting " treason to the Constitution," and preparing to " assail the Union it ordained and established "—a proper subject for his own denunciations.

[2] Mr. Breckinridge was then Vice-president of the United States under President Buchanan, and subsequent events show that he was a co-worker with Davis and others against the Government. He joined the insurgents, and, during a portion of the civil war that ensued, he was the so-called " Secretary of War " of Jefferson Davis.

summer-time of 1860. The respective friends of the opposing candidates of that party (STEPHEN A. DOUGLAS and JOHN C. BRECKINRIDGE) went into the canvass with great bitterness of feeling, such as family quarrels usually exhibit.

Six days after the adjournment of the *Democratic* Conventions at Charleston, representatives of a new political organization, not more than six months old, met in Convention at Baltimore.[*] They styled themselves the *National Constitutional Union Party*, composed almost wholly of members of the old *Whig* party and a waning organization known as the *American*, or *Know-nothing* party. They assembled in the First Presbyterian Meeting-house (known as the Two-steeple Church),

[* May 9, 1860.]

on Fayette Street, between Calvert and North Streets, which has since been demolished, and its place occupied by the United States Court-house. Its interior was well decorated with National emblems. Back of the president's chair was a full-length portrait of Washington, with large American flags, over which hovered an eagle; and the galleries, which were crowded with spectators, were festooned with numerous Union banners.

The venerable John J. Crittenden, of Kentucky, Chairman of the National Constitutional Union Committee, called the Convention to order, and on his nomination, Washington Hunt, once Governor of the State of New York, and distinguished for talent, culture, and great urbanity of manner, was chosen temporary president of the Convention. Credentials of delegates were called for, when it was found that almost one-third of all the States were unrepresented.[1]

THE FIRST PRESBYTERIAN CHURCH, BALTIMORE, IN 1860.

Toward evening, after a recess, Governor Hunt was elected permanent President. When the subject of a platform was proposed, Leslie Coombs, of Kentucky, an ardent follower and admirer of Henry Clay, took the floor, and put the Convention in the best of humor by a characteristic little speech. He declared that he had constructed three platforms: one for the "harmonious Democracy, who had agreed so beautifully, at Charleston;" another for the Republicans, about to assemble at Chicago; and a third for the party then around him. For the first, he proposed the Kentucky and Virginia Resolutions of 1798, which seemed to give license for the secession

---

[1] The States not represented were California, Florida, Iowa, Louisiana, Michigan, New Hampshire, Rhode Island, Oregon, South Carolina, and Wisconsin—ten in all.

of States, and disunion; for the second, the Blue-Laws of Connecticut; and for the third, the Constitution of the United States—"the Constitution as it is, and the Union under it, now and forever." The last sentence touched a  sympathetic chord in the Convention, of marvelous sensitiveness. The suggestion was received with the most enthusiastic demonstrations of delight; and on the second day of the session, Joseph R. Ingersoll, Chairman of the Committee on Platform, reported resolutions, which repudiated all creeds formed for a temporary purpose, as "calculated to mislead and deceive the people," and recommended, as a foundation for the party to plant itself upon in the coming contest, that which was defined by the words:—THE CONSTITUTION OF THE COUNTRY, THE

WASHINGTON HUNT.

UNION OF THE STATES, AND THE EN-FORCEMENT OF THE LAWS. This platform was adopted unanimously.

The Convention now proceeded to vote for candidates for the offices of President and Vice-president, when two hundred and fifty-four votes were cast; and on the second ballot, John Bell, of Tennessee, an eminent politician, then past sixty-three years of age, was nominated for the Presidency.[1] The renowned scholar, statesman, and diplomat, the late Edward Everett, of Massachusetts, was selected for the office of Vice-president. In the canvass that followed, the adherents of these gentlemen were popularly known as the *Bell-Everett* party.

The greatest harmony prevailed in this Convention. Not a word was said about "Americanism," or other old party issues, nor was there a whisper on the subject of Slavery, excepting an ejaculation of Neil S. Brown, of Tennessee, who thanked God that he had at last found a Convention in which the "nigger" was not the sole subject of consideration. The great topic for speech was the *Constitution*, which they thought would be imperiled by the election of either Douglas, Breckinridge, or the nominee of the Republican party, whoever he might be. The Convention adjourned on the second day of the session, and that night a ratification meeting was held in Monument Square, in Baltimore, whereat speakers and musicians were abundant. The spacious platform, erected in the Square, was spanned by an immense arch, on which were inscribed the words—"THE UNION, THE CONSTITUTION, AND THE ENFORCEMENT OF THE LAWS."

Six days after the adjournment of the *National Constitutional Union* Convention, the representatives of the Republican party assembled in large numbers at Chicago, Illinois—a city of more than one hundred thousand souls, on the verge of a prairie on the western shore of Lake Michigan, where, in 1830, there were only a small fort, and a few scattered houses of traders—a city

---

[1] When the Rebellion broke out, in the spring of 1861, Mr. Bell was one of the earliest, if not the very first, of the professed Unionists of distinction who joined the enemies of his country in their attempt to overthrow the Constitution and destroy the nationality of the Republic.

illustrious as one of the wonders of the growth of our Republic. All of the Free-labor States were fully represented, and there were delegates from several of the Slave-labor States. An immense building of boards, called a

WIGWAM AT CHICAGO, IN 1860.

Wigwam, had been erected by the Republicans of Chicago, at an expense of seven thousand dollars, for the special use of the Convention. It was tastefully decorated within, and was spacious enough to hold ten thousand persons. A rustic seat, made of a huge knot of a tree, was prepared for the use of the President of the Convention; and everything about the affair was rough and rural in appearance. The Convention met in the Wigwam, on the 16th day of May. Not more than one-third of the vast gathering of people could enter the building. E. D. Morgan, of New York, Chairman of the National Republican Executive Committee, called the Convention to order, and David Wilmot, of

PRESIDENT'S CHAIR.

Pennsylvania, was chosen temporary chairman. In due time, George Ashmun, of Massachusetts, was chosen permanent President. It was a wise choice. His voice could be heard above any clamor that might be raised in the assembly, and he was remarkable for coolness, clearness of judgment, and executive ability. He was presented with a gavel made of a piece of the oak timber of Perry's flag-ship, *Lawrence;* and with this emblem of authority, inscribed with the words, *"Don't give up the ship!"* he called the Convention to order, and invited the delegates to business. A committee on resolutions, composed of one delegate from each State represented, was appointed, and on the following morning[*] it submitted to the Convention a platform of principles, in the form of seventeen resolutions.   [* May 17, 1860.]

After affirming that the maintenance of the principles promulgated in the Declaration of Independence, and embodied in the National Constitution, is essential to the preservation of our republican institutions; congratulating the country that no Republican member of Congress had uttered or countenanced any threats of disunion, "so often made by Democratic members without rebuke, and with applause from their political associates," and denouncing such threats as "an avowal of contemplated treason," the resolutions made explicit declarations upon the topic of Slavery, so largely occupying public attention. In a few paragraphs, they declared that each State had the absolute right of control in the management of its own domestic concerns; that the new dogma that the Constitution, of its own force, carries Slavery into any or all of the Territories of the United States, was a dangerous political heresy, revolutionary in its tendency, and subversive of the peace and harmony of the country; that the normal condition of all the territory of the United States is that of freedom, and that neither Congress, nor a Territorial legislature, nor any individuals, have authority to give legal existence to Slavery in any Territory of the United States; and that the reopening of the African Slave-trade, then recently commenced in the Southern States, under the cover of our national flag, aided by perversions of judicial power, was a crime against humanity, and a burning shame to our country and age.

GEORGE ASHMUN.

This platform was adopted at six o'clock in the evening, by unanimous vote; when the Convention adjourned until next morning, without taking a ballot for candidates for the Presidency and Vice-presidency. When the . vote on the platform was announced, the scene that ensued, says an eye-witness, was of the "most astounding character. All the thousands of men in that enormous Wigwam commenced swinging their hats, and cheering with immense enthusiasm, and the other thousands of ladies waved their handkerchiefs and clapped their hands. Such a spectacle as was witnessed for some minutes has never before been witnessed at a convention. As the great assemblage poured through the streets after adjournment, it seemed to electrify the city. The agitation of the masses that packed the hotels and thronged the streets, certainly forty thousand strong, was such as made the little excitement at Charleston seem insignificant."[1]

* May 19, 1860.   On the morning of the third day of the session,* the Convention was opened with prayer, by the Rev. Mr. Green, of Chicago, who expressed a desire that the evils which then invested the body politic should be wholly eradicated from the system, and that the pen of the historian might trace an intimate connection between that "glorious consummation and the transactions of the Convention." Then that body proceeded to the choice of a Presidential candidate, and on the third ballot Abraham Lincoln, of Illinois, was nominated. The announcement of the result caused the most uproarious applause; and, from the common center at Chicago, the electric messengers flew with the intelligence, almost as quick as thought, to every part of the vast Republic, eastward of the Rocky Mountains, before sunset. The Convention took a recess, and in the evening nominated Hannibal Hamlin, of Maine, for Vice-president. Their labors

[1] Halstead's *History of the National Political Conventions in 1860*, page 139.

were now done, and, after a brief speech by their presiding officer, the Convention adjourned, with nine cheers for the ticket.

Mr. Lincoln, the nominee, was at his home in Springfield, Illinois, at this time. He had been in the telegraph-office during the first and second ballotings, when he left, went to the office of the *State Journal*, and was conversing with friends when the third balloting occurred. The result was known at Springfield a few minutes after the voting was finished. The superintendent of the telegraph there wrote on a scrap of paper, "Mr. Lincoln, you are nominated," and sent a boy with it to the nominee. Mr. Lincoln read it to his friends, and, while they huzzaed lustily, he looked at it in silence. Then, putting it quietly in his pocket, he bade them "good evening," and went home.[1]

On the following day, a committee, appointed by the Convention, with President Ashmun at their head, waited upon Mr. Lincoln, and formally communicated to him, orally, and by an official letter, the fact of his nomination. He received the message with great modesty and gravity, and promised to respond to it in writing. This he did three days afterward,[a] in which, after accepting the nomination, he said:— [a May 26, 1860.] "The declaration of principles and sentiments which accompanies your letter, meets my approval, and it shall be my care not to violate it, or disregard it in any part. Imploring the assistance of Divine Providence, and with due regard to the views and feelings of all who were represented in the Convention, to the rights of all the States and Territories and people of the nation, to the inviolability of the Constitution, and the perpetual union, harmony, and prosperity of all, I am most happy to co-operate for the practical success of the principles declared by the Convention."

In the beautiful month of June, when Nature, in the temperate zone, is most wealthy in flowers and foliage and the songs of birds, and there is every thing in her aspect to inspire delight, and harmony, and good-will, one of the most important political campaigns noted in history was opened with intense vigor, and the most uncompromising and relentless hostility of parties. There were four of these parties in the field of contest, namely :—

1. The *Republican*, who declared freedom to be the normal condition of all territory, and that Slavery can exist only by authority of municipal law. Of this party, Abraham Lincoln was the standard-bearer.

2. The wing of the Democratic party led by John C. Breckinridge, who declared that no power existed that might lawfully control Slavery in the Territories; that it existed in any Territory, in full force, whenever a slaveholder and his slaves entered it; and that it was the duty of the National Government to protect it there.

3. The wing of the Democratic party led by Stephen A. Douglas, whose platform of principles assumed not to know positively whether slavery might or might not have lawful existence in the Territories, without the action of the inhabitants thereof, but expressed a willingness to abide by the decisions of the Supreme Court in all cases.

4. The *National Constitutional Union* party, led by John Bell, who

---

1 "There is a little woman down at our house," said Mr. Lincoln, in allusion to his wife, as he left the room, "who would like to hear this—I'll go down and tell her."

declined to express any opinion upon any subject, but pointed to the National Constitution, without note or comment, as their political guide.

The politicians of only the two parties first named seemed to have positive convictions, as units, on the great subject which had so long agitated the nation, and they took issue squarely, definitely, and defiantly. A large portion of the Douglas party were also inclined to disregard the resolution which bound them to absolute submission to the decisions of the Supreme Court, and to stand firmly upon a pure "Popular Sovereignty" Platform, which that resolution had eviscerated, for they regarded a late decision of the majority of that court, in the case of Dred Scott,[1] as sufficiently indicative of its opposition to the great doctrine of that platform. All parties were agreed in earnest professions of love for the Union and the Constitution; and, with such avowals emblazoned on their standards, they went into the fight, each doubtful of success, and all conscious that a national crisis was at hand. There was a vague presentiment before the minds of reflecting men everywhere, that the time when the practical answer to the great question—What shall be the policy of the Nation concerning Slavery?—could no longer be postponed.

The conflict was desperate from July to November, and grew more intense as it approached its culmination at the polls. The Republicans and Douglas Democrats were denounced by their opponents as Abolitionists—treasonably sectional, and practically hostile to the perpetuation of the Union. The Breckinridge party, identified as it unfortunately was with avowed disunionists—men who for long years had been in the habit of threatening to attempt the dissolution of the Union by the process of secession, whenever the revelations of the Census or other causes should convince them that the domination of the Slave interest in the National Government had ceased forever—men who rejoiced when they saw, in the absolute disruption of the Democratic party at Charleston and Baltimore, a prospect for the election of the Republican candidate, which might serve them as a pretext for rebellion—men who afterward became leaders in the great insurrection against the National Government—was charged with complicity in disunion schemes. In speeches, newspapers, and in social gatherings, these charges were iterated and reiterated; and yet there were but few persons in the Free-labor States who really believed that there were men mad enough and wicked enough to raise the arm of resistance to the authority of the Supreme Government, founded on the National Constitution.

But the election of Mr. Lincoln, which was the result of the great political conflict in the summer and autumn of 1860, soon revealed the existence of a well-organized conspiracy against the life of the Republic, widespread, powerful, and intensely malignant. The leading conspirators were few, and nearly all of them were then, or had been, connected with the

---

[1] Dred Scott had been a slave in Missouri, but claimed to be a freeman on account of involuntary residence in a free State. The case did not require a decision concerning the right of a negro to citizenship; but the Chief-Justice took the occasion to give what is called an extra-judicial opinion. He decided that a freed negro slave, or a descendant of a slave, could not become a citizen of the Republic. He asserted, in that connection, that the language of the Declaration of Independence showed that the negroes were not included in the benefiwent meaning of that Instrument, when it said, "*all* men are created equal," and that they were regarded "as so far inferior, that they had no rights which the white man was bound to respect."

National Government, some as legislators, and others as cabinet ministers. They were not so numerous at first, according to a loyal Tennessean (Horace Maynard), who knew them well, "as the figures on a chess-board," but became wonderfully productive of their kind. "There are those," he said, in a speech in Congress, "within reach of my voice, who also know them, and can testify to their utter perfidy; who have been the victims of their want of principle, and whose self-respect has suffered from their insolent and overbearing demeanor. No Northern man was ever admitted to their confidence, and no Southern man, unless it became necessary to keep up their numbers; and then, not till he was thoroughly known by them, and known to be thoroughly corrupt. They, like a certain school of ancient philosophers, had two sets of principles or doctrines—one for outsiders, the other for themselves; the one was 'Democratic principles' for the Democratic party, the other was their own and without a name. Some Northern men and many Southern men were, after a fashion, petted and patronized by them, as a gentleman throws from his table a bone, or a choice bit, to a favorite dog; and they imagined they were conferring a great favor thereby, which could be requited only by the abject servility of the dog. To hesitate, to doubt, to hold back, to stop, was to call down a storm of wrath that few men had the nerve to encounter, and still fewer the strength to withstand. Not only in political circles, but in social life, their rule was inexorable, their tyranny absolute. God be thanked for the brave men who had the courage to meet them and bid them defiance, first at Charleston, in April, 1860, and then at Baltimore, in June! To them is due the credit of declaring war against this intolerable despotism." The truthfulness of this picture will be fully apparent in future pages.

CHAPTER II.

PRELIMINARY REBELLIOUS MOVEMENTS.

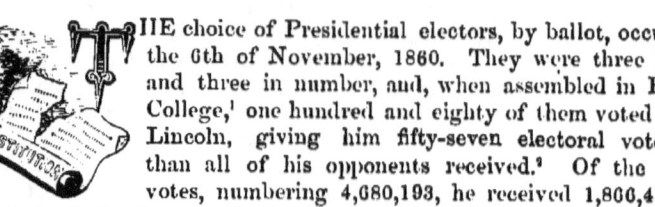

THE choice of Presidential electors, by ballot, occurred on the 6th of November, 1860. They were three hundred and three in number, and, when assembled in Electoral College,[1] one hundred and eighty of them voted for Mr. Lincoln, giving him fifty-seven electoral votes more than all of his opponents received.[2] Of the popular votes, numbering 4,680,193, he received 1,866,452. Although he had a large majority over each candidate, he received 979,103 less than did all of his opponents.[3] This fact, and the circumstance that in nine Slave-labor States there was no Republican electoral ticket, gave factitious vigor to the plausible cry, which was immediately raised by the conspirators and their friends, that the President elect would be a usurper when in office, because he had not received a majority of the aggregate vote of the people; that he would be a sectional ruler, and, of necessity, a tyrant; and that his antecedents, the principles of the Republican platform, and the fanaticism of his supporters, pledged him to wage relentless war upon the system of Slavery, and the rights of the Slave-labor States.

It was not denied that Mr. Lincoln had been elected in accordance with the letter and spirit of the National Constitution,[4] and that it was the fault of the politicians in the nine States that there were no electoral tickets therein.[5] Many of these politicians began at once, with intense zeal, which often amounted to ferocity, to put in motion a system of terrorism, in which the hangman's rope, the incendiary's torch, and the slave-hunter's blood-hound, formed prominent features. It was often perilous to his life and property, for a man below North Carolina and Tennessee to express a desire for Mr. Lincoln's election. The promise of a United States Senator from North Carolina (Clingman), that Union men would be hushed by "the swift attention of vigilance committees," was speedily fulfilled.

It was not denied that the election had been fairly and legally conducted, or that the Republican platform pledged the nominee and his supporters to absolute non-interference with the rights and domestic policy of the States. That platform expressly declared, that "the maintenance, inviolate, of the rights of the States, and especially the right of each State to order and con-

---

[1] See Article XII. of the Amendments to the Constitution.

[2] Bell received 39, Douglas 12, and Breckinridge 72.

[3] He received 491,295 over Douglas, 1,018,499 over Breckinridge, and 1,275,821 over Bell. The votes for the four candidates, respectively, were: For Lincoln, 1,866,452; for Bell, 590,631; for Douglas, 1,375,144; and for Breckinridge, 847,953.

[4] See Article XII. of the Amendments to the Constitution.

[5] These were North Carolina, Georgia, Alabama, Mississippi, Tennessee, Louisiana, Arkansas, Florida, and Texas. The electors of South Carolina were chosen by the State Legislature.

trol its own domestic institutions according to its own judgment, is essential to that balance of power on which the perfection and endurance of our political fabric depend." But these and other facts, essential to a correct understanding of the issue, were studiously concealed from the people, or so adroitly shrouded in sophistry that they were kept far away from popular cognizance.

During the canvass preceding the election, the conspirators, and the politicians in their train, employed all the means in their power to excite intensely every blinding passion of the slaveholders and the masses of the people. They appealed to their fears, their prejudices, their local patriotism, and their greed. They asserted, with all the solemn seeming of sober truth, that the people of the Free-labor States, grown rich and powerful through robbery of the people of the Slave-labor States, by means of tariff laws and other governmental measures, and by immigration from foreign lands, had elected a sectional President for the purpose of carrying out a long-cherished scheme of ambition, namely, the political and social subjugation of the inhabitants of the Slave-labor States; the subversion of their system of labor; the elevation of the negro to social equality with the white man; and the destruction of Slavery, upon which, they alleged, had rested in the past, and must forever rest in the future, all substantial prosperity in the cotton-growing States. They held the Republican party responsible for John Brown's acts at Harper's Ferry,[1] and declared that his raid was the forerunner of a general and destructive invasion of the Slave-labor States by "the fanatical hordes of the North." They cited the publications and speeches of the Abolitionists of the North during the past thirty years; the legislation in the same section unfriendly to slavery; and the more recent utterances of leading members of the Republican party, in which it had been declared that "there is an irrepressible conflict between freedom and slavery"—"the Republic cannot exist half slave and half free"—"freedom is the normal condition of all territory," &c.; they cited these with force, as proofs of long and earnest preparation for a now impending war upon "the South" and its institutions. They pictured, in high coloring, the dreadful paralysis of all the industry and commerce of "the South," and the utter extinguishment of all hopes of future advancement in art, science, literature, and the development of the yet hidden resources in the region below the Susquehanna, the Potomac, and the Ohio, as a consequence of the domination in the National Government of their "bitter enemies," as they unjustly termed the people of the Free-labor States.[2]

In this unholy work, the press and the pulpit became powerful auxili-

---

[1] For the purpose of liberating the slaves of Virginia, John Brown, an enthusiast, with a few followers, seized Harper's Ferry, at the confluence of the Potomac and Shenandoah Rivers, in October, 1859, as a base of operations. He failed. He was arrested by National and Virginia troops, and was hanged, in December following, by the authorities of Virginia.

[2] This false teaching was not new. It was begun by John C. Calhoun, and had been kept up ever since. It was so in Madison's later days. In a letter to Henry Clay, cited by Dr. Sargeant, in his admirable pamphlet, entitled, *England, the United States, and the Southern Confederacy,* that statesman and patriot said:—" It is painful to see the unceasing efforts made to alarm the South, by imputations against the North of unconstitutional designs on the subject of Slavery." Madison and Clay were both slaveholders. Again, the former wrote: " The inculcated impression of a permanent incompatibility of interests between the North and the South *may put it in the power of popular leaders, aspiring to the highest stations,* to unite the South on some critical occasion. In pursuing this course, the first and most obvious step is nullification, the next secession, and the last, a final separation."

aries. The former was widely controlled by politicians of the small ruling class in the Slave-labor States, and was almost everywhere subservient to their will in the promulgation of false teachings. There were exceptions, however—

W. G. BROWNLOW.

noble exceptions; and there were those among influential newspaper conductors, like the heroic "Parson Brownlow," of Knoxville, East Tennessee, now (1865) Governor of that State, who could never be brought to bend the knee a single line to Baal nor to Moloch; but stood bravely erect until consumed, as it were, at the stake of martyrdom.[1]

So with the pulpit. It was extensively occupied by men identified socially and pecuniarily with the slave system. These men, with the awful dignity of ambassadors of Christ—vicegerents of the Almighty—declared Slavery to be a "divine institution," and that the fanatics of the Free-labor States who denounced it as wrong and sinful were infidels, and deserved the fate of heretics. They joined their potential voices with those of the politicians, in the cry for resistance to expected wrong and oppression;[2] and thousands upon thousands of men and women, regarding them as oracles of wisdom and truth, followed them reverentially in the broad highway of open treason.[3]

---

[1] For an account of Dr. Brownlow's sufferings at the beginning of the war, see his work, entitled, *Sketches of the Rise, Progress, and Decline of Secession; with a Narrative of Personal Adventures among the Rebels.* G. W. Childs. 1862.

[2] See *The Church and the Rebellion*, by R. L. Stanton, D. D., of Kentucky.

[3] The change in the sentiments of the clergy in the Slave-labor States, during the twenty-five years preceding the war, was most remarkable. We will notice only two or three instances in a single religious body, namely, the Presbyterians. In 1835, the representatives of that denomination in South Carolina and Georgia, in Convention assembled, made an official report against the perpetuation of the system of Slavery. "We cannot go into detail," they said; "It is unnecessary. We make our appeal to universal experience. We are chained to a putrid carcass. It sickens and destroys us. We have a millstone about the neck of our society to sink us deep in the sea of vice. Our children are corrupted from their infancy, nor can we prevent it," &c.

In November, 1860, one of the most eminent Doctors of Divinity in the Presbyterian Church said, in his pulpit in New Orleans, after speaking of the character of the South:—"The particular trust assigned to such a people becomes the pledge of the Divine protection, and their fidelity to it determines the fate by which it is finally overtaken. What that trust is, must be ascertained from the necessities of their position, the institutions which are the outgrowth of their principles, and the conflicts through which they preserve their identity and independence. If then the South is such a people, what, at this juncture, is their providential trust? I answer, that it is *to conserve and to perpetuate the institution of domestic Slavery as now existing.*" Again: "I simply say, that for us, as now situated, the duty is plain of conserving and transmitting the system of Slavery, with the freest scope for its natural development and extension." Again: "Need I pause to show how this system is interwoven with our entire social fabric? That these slaves form parts of our households, even as our children; and that, too, through a relationship recognized and sanctioned in the Scriptures of God, even as the other? Must I pause to show how it has fashioned our modes of life, and determined all our habits of thought and feeling, and molded the very type of our civilization? How then can the hand of violence be laid upon it, without involving our existence?"—*The South, her Peril and her Duty: a Thanksgiving Discourse*, Nov. 29, 1860, by Rev. B. M. Palmer, D. D.

Ten or fifteen years before the war, an eminent Doctor of Divinity of the Presbyterian Church, in Charleston, South Carolina, put forth two pamphlets, in which he sought to claim for that denomination the glory of the authorship of the Declaration of Independence, alleging that its form and substance were fashioned after the bands and covenants of the church in Scotland. "Presbyterianism," he says exultingly, in praising the Declaration of Independence as almost divine in origin and character, "has proved itself to be the pillar and ground of truth, amid error and defection. It has formed empires, in the spirit of Freedom and Liberty, and has given birth to declarations and achievements which *are the wonder of the present, and will*

The "common people"—the non-slaveholders and the small slaveholders—whom the ruling class desired to reduce to vassalage,[1] but to whom they now looked for physical aid in the war which their madness might kindle, were blinded, confused, and alarmed. They were assured that the independence of the South would bring riches and honor to every household. They were deluded with promises of free trade, that would bring the luxuries of the world to their dwellings. They were promised the long-desired reopening of the African Slave-trade, which would make slaves so cheap that every man might become an owner of many, and take his position in the

---

be the admiration of every future age." On the 21st of November, 1860, the same Doctor of Divinity said, from the pulpit of the Second Presbyterian Church in Charleston, after stating that he stood there "in God's name and stead, to point out the cause of His anger:"—"Now, to me, pondering long and profoundly upon the course of events, the evil and bitter root of all our evils is to be found in the infidel, atheistic, French Revolution, Red Republican principle, embodied as an axiomatic seminal principle—not in the Constitution, but in the Declaration of Independence. That seminal principle is this:—'We hold these truths to be self-evident: that all men are created equal; that they are endowed by their Creator with certain inalienable rights; that among these are life, liberty, and the pursuit of happiness.'"—The Sin and the Cure, by Rev. Thomas Smyth, D. D.

Doctor James H. Thornwell, President of a Theological Seminary at Columbia, S. C., one of the most eminent scholars and theologians in the South, and who was known in that State as "The Calhoun of the Church," was ever foremost in the defense of Slavery as a divine institution. He even went so far as to assert his conviction that the horrible African Slave-trade was "the most worthy of all Missionary Societies." Clergymen of every religious denomination in the Slave-labor States were involved in the crime of rebellion, for the sake of perpetuating human Slavery. Their speeches, and sermons, and recorded acts are full of evidence that the Church, in the broad meaning of that term, had become horribly corrupted by the Slave system, and made a willing instrument of the conspirators. It is related by the Rev. Dr. Stanton (The Church and the Rebellion, p. 163), that Robert Toombs, of Georgia, an arch-conspirator, went early to New Orleans, to stir up the people to revolt. The Union sentiment was too strong for him, and he was about to leave, when it was suggested that the Rev. Dr. Palmer might be induced to preach a new gospel, whose chief tenet should be the righteousness of Slavery. He seems to have been very ready to do so, and the Fast-day Sermon of Dr. Palmer, above alluded to, with all its terrible results, was a part of the fruits of the mission of Toombs to New Orleans, in the autumn of 1860.

Dr. Palmer's discourse was seditious throughout. It was printed, and circulated by thousands all over the Slave-labor States, with direful effect. In the summer of 1865, after the war was ended, Dr. Palmer entered the same pulpit, and "frankly told his people," says a New Orleans correspondent of the Boston Post, "that they had all been wrong, and he 'the chief of sinners;' that they had been proud and haughty, disobedient, rebellious; that he himself had been humbled before God, and received merited chastisement; that they had all been taught a good lesson of obedience to civil authority, and he hoped it would be filially received by them as the children of Christ, and laid up in their heart of hearts."

For a complete history of the change in the sentiments of Christians of all denominations in the Slave-labor States, and the relations of the clergy to the conspirators, see a volume entitled The Church and the Rebellion, by R. L. Stanton, D. D., of Kentucky.

[1] Of the 12,000,000 of inhabitants in the Slave-labor States, at the beginning of the war, the ruling class—those in whom resided, in a remarkable degree, the political power of the States—numbered about 1,000,000, . Of these, the large land and slave holders, whose influence in the body of the million named was almost supreme, numbered less than 200,000. "In 1850," says Edward Atkinson, in the Continental Monthly for March, 1862, page 252, "there were in all the Southern States less than 170,000 men owning more than five slaves each, and they owned 2,500,000 out of 3,300,000." The production of the great staple, cotton, which was regarded as king of kings in an earthly sense, was in the hands of less than 100,000 men.

The remaining 11,000,000 of inhabitants in the Slave-labor States consisted of 6,000,000 of small slaveholders and non-slaveholders, mechanics, and laboring men; 4,000,000 of negro slaves, and 1,000,000 known in those regions by the common name of "poor white trash," a degraded population scattered over the whole surface of these States. The foregoing figures are only proximately exact, but may be relied on as a truthful statement of statistics, in round numbers.

For several years preceding the rebellion, many of the leading publicists in the Slave-labor States openly advocated a form of government radically opposed to that of our Republic. Their chief vehicle of communication with the small ruling class in those States was De Bow's Review, a magazine of much pretension and of acknowledged authority. The following brief paragraphs from the pages of that periodical, selected from a thousand of like tenor, will serve to illustrate the truth of the assertion in the text, that the vassalage of the "common people," in the new empire which long-contemplated revolt was to establish, was intended:—

"The right to govern resides in a very small minority; the duty to obey is inherent in the great mass of mankind."

"There is nothing to which the South [the ruling class] entertains so great a dislike as of universal suffrage. Wherever foreigners settle together in large numbers, there universal suffrage will exist. They understand and admire the leveling democracy of the North, but cannot appreciate the aristocratic feeling of a privileged class, so universal at the South."

"The real civilization of a country is in its aristocracy. The masses are molded into soldiers and artisans by intellect, just as matter and the elements of nature are made into telegraphs and steam-engines. The poor,

social scale, with the great proprietors of lands and sinews.[1] Every avenue through which truth might find its way to the popular understanding was quickly closed, and the people had no detecter of its counterfeits. "Perhaps there never was a people," wrote a Southern Unionist, in the third year of the war, "more bewitched, beguiled, and befooled than we were when we drifted into this rebellion."[2]

Commenting on these actions of the politicians, President Lincoln said:— "At the beginning, they knew they would never raise their treason to any respectable magnitude by any name which implies violation of law. They knew their people possessed as much moral sense, as much of devotion to law and order, and as much pride in, and reverence for, the history and Government of their common country, as any other civilized and patriotic people. They knew they would make no advancement directly in the teeth of these strong and noble sentiments. Accordingly, they commenced by an insidious debauching of the public mind. They invented an ingenious sophism, which, if conceded, was followed by perfectly logical steps, through all the incidents, to the complete destruction of the Union. The sophism itself is, that any State of the Union may, consistently with the National Constitution, and therefore lawfully and peacefully, withdraw from the Union, without the consent of the Union, or of any other State. The little disguise that the supposed right is to be exercised only for just cause, themselves to be the judges of its justice, is too thin to merit any notice. With rebellion thus sugarcoated, they have been drugging the public mind of their section for more than thirty years, until, at length, they have brought many good men to a willingness to take up arms against the Government, the day after some assemblage of men have enacted the farcical pretense of taking their State out of the Union, who could have been brought to no such thing the day before."[3]

who labor all day, are too tired at night to study books. If you make them learned, they soon forget all that is necessary in the common transactions of life. To make an aristocrat in the future, *we must sacrifice a thousand paupers.* Yet we would by all means make them—make them permanent, too, by laws of entail and primogeniture. An aristocracy is patriarchal, parental, and representative. The feudal barons of England were, next to the fathers, the most perfect representative government. The king and barons represented everybody, because *everybody belonged to them.*"

And when the war broke out, a writer in the *Review* said, with truth and candor:—"The real contest of to-day is not simply between the North and South; but to determine whether for ages to come our Government shall partake more of the form of monarchies or of more liberal forms."

[1] There is ample evidence on record to show that Yancey, Davis, Stephens, and other leaders in the great rebellion were advocates of the foreign slave-trade. Southern newspapers advocated it. The *True Southron*, of Mississippi, suggested the "propriety of stimulating the zeal of the pulpit by founding a prize *for the best sermon in favor of free trade in negroes.*" For the purpose of practically opening the horrible traffic, an "African Labor-supply Association" was formed, of which De Bow, editor of the principal organ of the oligarchy, was made president. Southern legislatures discussed the question. John Slidell, in the United States Senate, urged the propriety of withdrawing American cruisers from the coast of Africa, that the slavers might not be molested; and the administration of Mr. Buchanan was made to favor this scheme of the great cotton-planters, by protesting against the visitation of suspected slave-bearing vessels, carrying the American flag, by British cruisers.

[2] *New York Daily Times*, June 4, 1864.

[3] Message to Congress, July 4, 1861. Mr. Carpenter, the artist who painted the picture of *The Signing of the Emancipation Proclamation*, relates the following anecdote concerning the last sentence in the above quotation from the Message:—"Mr. De Frees, the Government printer, told me that when the Message was being printed, he was a good deal disturbed by the use of the term 'sugar-coated,' and finally went to the President about it. Their relations to each other being of the most intimate character, he told Mr. Lincoln frankly that he ought to remember that a message to Congress was a different affair from a speech at a mass meeting in Illinois—that the messages became a part of history, and should he written accordingly. 'What is the matter now?' inquired the President. 'Why,' said Mr. De Frees, 'you have used an undignified expression in the Message;' and then reading the paragraph aloud, he added, ' I would alter the structure of that, if I were you.' 'De Frees,' replied Mr. Lincoln, 'that word expresses precisely my idea, and I am not going to change it. The time will never come, in this country, when the people won't know exactly what *sugar-coated* means!'"

During the summer and early autumn of 1860, William L. Yancey, one of the most active and influential of the conspirators, with other disunionists, made a pilgrimage through the Free-labor States, for the purpose of vindicating the claims put forth by the extremists of the South, concerning State supremacy and the unrestricted extension of Slavery. They were listened to patiently by thousands at public meetings; were hospitably treated everywhere; received assurances of sympathy from vast numbers of men who regarded the agitation of the Slavery question, by the Abolitionists, as mischievous, unfriendly, and dangerous to the peace of the Union; and then they went back, with treason in their hearts and falsehoods upon their lips, to deceive and arouse into rebellion the masses of the Southern people, who regarded them as oracles. Like an incar-

WILLIAM L. YANCEY.

nation of Discord, Yancey cried, substantially as he had written two years before:—" Organize committees all over the Cotton States; fire the Southern heart; instruct the Southern mind; give courage to each other; and at the proper moment, by one organized, concerted action, precipitate the Cotton States into revolution."[1]

This advice was instantly followed when the election of Mr. Lincoln was assured by the decision of the ballot-box, on the 6th of November. Indeed, before that decision was made, South Carolina conspirators—disciples and political successors of John C. Calhoun[2]—met at the house of James

---

[1] Letter to James Slaughter, June 15, 1858.

[2] John Caldwell Calhoun, of South Carolina, always appears in history as the central figure of a group of politicians who, almost forty years ago, adopting the disunion theories put forth by a few Virginians, like John Taylor, of Caroline, and used by Jefferson and his friends for the temporary purpose of securing a political party victory at the close of the last century, began, in more modern times, the work of destroying the nationality of the Republic. With amazing intellectual vigor and acumen, Mr. Calhoun crystallized the crude elements of opposition to that nationality, found in so great abundance, as we have observed, in Virginia, during Washington's Administration, that it drew from him his great plea for union in his Farewell Address to his countrymen. Calhoun reduced these elements to compact form, and, by the consummate use of the most subtle sophistry, of which he was complete master, he instilled the most dangerous disintegrating poison, known as the doctrine of Supreme State Sovereignty, into the public mind of the Slave-labor States, for the purpose of meeting a contingency which he contemplated as early as the year 1812. The now [1865] venerable Rear-admiral Stewart, in a letter to George W. Childs, of Philadelphia, relates a conversation between himself and Mr. Calhoun, in Washington City, in the winter of 1812:—" You in the South," said Stewart, "are decidedly the aristocratic portion of this Union; you are so, in holding persons in perpetual slavery; you are so, in every domestic quality; so in every habit of your lives, modes of living, and action. You neither work with your hands, head, nor any machinery, but live and have your being, not in accordance with the will of your Creator, but by the sweat of slavery; and yet you assume all the attributes, professions, and advantages of Democracy." Mr. Calhoun replied:—" I admit your conclusions in respect to us Southerners. That we are essentially aristocratic, I cannot deny. But we can, and do, yield much to Democracy. *This is our sectional policy.* We are, from necessity, thrown upon and solemnly wedded to that party, however it may occasionally clash with our feelings, for the conservation of our interests. It is through our affiliation with that party, in the Middle and Western States, that we hold power. *But when we cease thus to control this nation, through a disjointed Democracy, or any material obstacle in that party shall tend to throw us out of that rule and control, we shall resort to a dissolution of the Union. The compromises of the Constitution, under the circumstances, were sufficient for our fathers; but under the altered condition of our country, from that period, leave to the South no resource but dissolution.*"

This avowal of Mr. Calhoun, then a leading Democratic member of Congress, that the politicians of the South were determined to rule the Republic, or ruin it, was made forty-eight years before the great rebellion occurred. Under the lead of Calhoun, the politicians of South Carolina attempted a rebellion about thirty years before, but failed.

II. Hammond (son of a New England schoolmaster, and an extensive land and slave holder, near the banks of the Savannah River), to consult upon a plan of treasonable operations. Hammond was then a member of the United States Senate, pledged by solemn oath to see that the Republic received no hurt; and yet, under his roof, he met in conclave a band of

JOHN CALDWELL CALHOUN.

men, like himself sworn to be defenders of his native land, from foes without and foes within, to plot schemes for the ruin of that country. At his table, and in secret session in his library, sat William H. Gist, then Governor of South Carolina; ex-governor James H. Adams; James L. Orr, once Speaker of the National House of Representatives; the entire Congressional Delegation of South Carolina,[1] excepting William Porcher Miles (who was compelled by sickness to be absent), and several other prominent men of that State. Then and there the plan for the overt act of rebellion, performed by South Carolinians in Convention at Charleston, sixty days later, seems to have been arranged. They were assured that their well-managed sundering of the Democratic party at Charleston, in April,[2] would result in the election of Mr. Lincoln, and that the pretext for rebellion, so long and anxiously waited for, would be presented within a fortnight from that time.

This meeting was followed by similar cabals in the other cotton-growing States; and, in Virginia, that ever-restless mischief-maker, ex-governor Henry A. Wise, with R. M. T. Hunter, John Tyler, James M. Mason, the author of the Fugitive Slave Law of 1850, who had been his co-plotter against the life of the Republic four years before,[3] and other leading politicians in that State, were exceedingly active in arranging plans for that Commonwealth to join her Southern sisters in the work of treason. Wise, who assumed to be their orator on all occasions, had openly declared, that

---

[1] These were John McQueen, Lawrence M. Keitt, Milledge L. Bonham, John D. Ashmore, and William W. Boyce, of the House of Representatives, and Senators James H. Hammond and James Chesnut, Jr.

[2] See page 23.

[3] In response to an invitation from Wise, a convention of Governors of Slave-labor States was secretly held at Raleigh, North Carolina, of which Jefferson Davis, then the Secretary of War, was fully cognizant. The object was to devise a scheme of rebellion at that time, in the event of the election of Colonel John C. Frémont, the Republican candidate for the Presidency. Wise afterward boasted that, had Frémont been elected, he should have marched, at the head of twenty thousand men, to Washington, taken possession of the Capitol, and prevented the inauguration of the President elect. Frémont's defeat postponed overt acts of treason by the conspirators.—*The American Conflict:* by Horace Greeley, i. 329. Senator Mason, writing to Jeff. Davis on the 30th of September, said:—" I have a letter from Wise, of the 27th, full of spirit. He says the governments of North Carolina, South Carolina, and Louisiana have already agreed to the *rendezvous* at Raleigh, and others will—this in your *most private ear*. He says further, that he had officially requested you to exchange with Virginia, on fair terms of difference, percussion for flint muskets. I don't know the usage or power of the Department in such cases; but, if it can be done, even by liberal construction, I hope you will accede. Was there not an appropriation at the last session for converting flint into percussion arms? If so, would it not furnish good reason for extending such facilities to the States? Virginia probably has more arms than the other Southern States, and would divide, in case of need. In a letter, yesterday, to a committee in South Carolina, I gave it as my judgment, in the event of Frémont's election, the South should not pause, but proceed at once to 'immediate, absolute, and eternal separation.' So I am a candidate for the first halter."

if Lincoln was elected, he " would not remain in the Union one hour."   He applauded, as hopeful words for his class, the declaration of Howell Cobb (then President Buchanan's Secretary of the Treasury), at a public gathering in the city of New York, that, in the event of Mr. Lincoln's election, secession would have the "sympathy and co-operation of the Administration," and that he "did not believe another Congress of the United States would meet." He hailed with delight, as chivalrous to the last degree, the assurances of Lawrence M. Keitt, of the House of Representatives, in a public speech, at Washington, that President Buchanan was "pledged to secession, and would be held to it;" that "South Carolina would shatter the accursed Union," and that, if she could not accomplish it otherwise, "she would throw her arms round the pillars of the Constitution, and involve all the States in a common ruin." He listened with peculiar pleasure to the declaration of Robert Barnwell Rhett, also of South Carolina, that "all true statesmanship in the

HENRY A. WISE.

South consists in forming combinations and shaping events, so as to bring about, as speedily as possible, a dissolution of the present Union, and a Southern Confederacy."—"Rather than submit one moment to Black Republican rule," Wise wrote to an old friend of his father, in the North, " I would fight to the last drop of blood to resist its fanatical oppression. Our minds are made up. *The South will not wait until the 4th of March. We will be well under arms before then*, or our safety must be guaranteed."[1]

Everywhere the conspirators and their followers and agents were sleepless in vigilance and tireless in energy. Hundreds of telegraphic messages, volumes of letters, and scores of couriers, went from plantation to plantation, from village to village, from city to city, and from State to State, wherever the Slave power held sway, stirring up the people to revolt; whilst prominent individuals and public bodies hastened, on hearing of the result of the election, to swell the grand chorus of treasonable speech, led by the dozen—they were but a little more in number—of the chief conspirators.[2]

Three, if not four, of these chief conspirators were President Buchanan's cabinet ministers and constitutional advisers. The three were Howell Cobb, of Georgia, Secretary of the Treasury; John B. Floyd, of Virginia, Secretary of War; and Jacob Thompson, of Mississippi, Secretary of the Interior. William H. Trescot, of South Carolina, who for many years had

---

[1] Autograph letter to Josiah Williams, of Poughkeepsie, N. Y., dated "Rolleston, near Norfolk, Va., December 24, 1860." Governor Wise, it will be remembered, was chiefly instrumental in procuring the execution of John Brown for treason, less than a year before. Four years later, his estate of "Rolleston, near Norfolk," was occupied as a camp for freed negroes; and, in his mansion, a daughter of John Brown was teaching colored children how to read and write the English language.

[2] See the remarks of Horace Maynard, on page 35.

been plotting against the life of the nation, was then Assistant Secretary of State, and their confederate in crime. These men, while in office, and pledged by solemn oaths to support the National Constitution and laws, were for months plotting schemes for the destruction of the former and defiance of the latter.

HOWELL COBB.

^{December 6, 1860.} From his official desk at Washington, Cobb wrote* an inflammatory address to the people of Georgia, in which he said, in conclusion :—" On the 4th of March, 1861, the Federal Government will pass into the hands of the Abolitionists. It will then cease to have the slightest claim either upon your confidence or your loyalty ; and, in my honest judgment, each hour that Georgia remains thereafter a member of the Union will be an hour of degradation, to be followed by certain and speedy ruin. I entertain no doubt either of your right or duty to secede from the Union. Arouse, then, all your manhood for the great work before you, and be prepared, on that day, to announce and maintain your independence of the Union, for you will never again have equality and justice in it. Identified with you in heart, feeling, and interest, I return to share in whatever destiny the future has ^{December 8, 1860.} in store for our State and ourselves." Two days afterward,* Cobb resigned his office,[1] hastened to Georgia, and afterward took up arms against his country.[2]

---

[1] In his letter to Mr. Buchanan, resigning his office, Mr. Cobb frankly informed him that duty to his State required him to sever his connection with the National Government, and lend his powers for the good of his own people. " I have prepared," he said, " and must now issue to them an address, which contains the calm and solemn convictions of my heart and judgment." As his views would, if he remained in the Cabinet, expose himself to suspicion, and put the President in a false position, he thought it proper to resign. In this, Mr. Cobb was more honest and honorable than his traitorous associates in the Cabinet, who remained almost a month longer.

[2] Cobb's plans had been matured before the election of Mr. Lincoln. So early as the 1st of November, 1860, Trescott, the Assistant Secretary of State, wrote to the editor of the *Charleston Mercury*, as follows :—

"WASHINGTON, Nov. 1, 1860.

"DEAR RHETT: I received your letter this morning. As to my views or opinions of the Administration, I can, of course, say nothing. As to Mr. Cobb's views, he is willing that I should communicate them to you, in order that they may aid you in forming your own judgment; but, you will understand that this is confidential —that is, neither Mr. Cobb nor myself must be quoted as the source of your information. I will not dwell on this, as you will, on a moment's reflection, see the embarrassment which might be produced by any *authorized* statement of his opinions. I will only add, by way of preface, that after the very fullest and freest conversations with him, I feel sure of his earnestness, singleness of purpose, and resolution in the whole matter.

"Mr. Cobb believes that the time is come for resistance; that upon the election of Lincoln, Georgia ought to secede from the Union, and that she will do so. That Georgia and every other State should, as far as secession, act for herself, resuming her delegated powers, and thus put herself in position to consult with other sovereign States who take the same ground. After the secession is effected, then will be the time to consult. But he is of opinion, most strongly, that whatever action is resolved on, should be consummated on the 4th of March, not before. That while the action determined on should be decisive and irrevocable, its initial point should be the 4th of March. He is opposed to any Southern convention, merely for the purpose of consultation. If a Southern convention is held, it must be of delegates empowered to *act*, whose action is at once binding on the States they represent.

"But he desires me to impress upon you his conviction, that any attempt to precipitate the actual issue upon this Administration will be most mischievous—calculated to produce differences of opinion and destroy

Floyd's treachery consisted more in secret, efficient action than in open words. As we shall observe presently, he had used the power of his official station to strip the arsenals of the Free-labor States of arms and ammunition, and to crowd those of the Slave-labor States with these materials of war; while Thompson, for more than ten years an avowed disunionist, was now plotting treason, it seems, by night and by day. He wrote from his official desk at Washington, as early as the 20th of November:—"My allegiance is due to Mis-

JACOB THOMPSON.

sissippi¹ and her destiny. I believe she ought to resist, and to the bitter end, Black Republican rule. . . . As long as I am here, I shall shield and protect the South. Whenever it shall come to pass that I think I can do no further good here, I shall return to my home. Buchanan is the truest friend to the South I have ever known in the North. He is a jewel of a man." After speaking of the intended secession of Mississippi, he said :— "I want the co-operation of the Southern States. I wish to do all I can to secure their sympathy and co-operation. A confederacy of the Southern States will be strong enough to command the respect of the world, and the love and confidence of our people at home. South Carolina will go. I consider Georgia and Florida as certain. Alabama probable. Then Mississippi must go. But I want Louisiana, Texas, Arkansas, Tennessee, North Carolina, Virginia; and Maryland will not stay behind long. . . . As soon as our mechanics, our merchants, our lawyers, our editors, look this matter in the face, and calculate the consequences, they will see their in-

unanimity. *He thinks it of great importance that the cotton crop should go forward at once, and that the money should be in the hands of the people, that the cry of popular distress shall not be heard at the outset of this more.**

"My own opinion is, that it would be well to have a discreet man, one who knows the value of silence, who can listen wisely, present in Milledgeville, at the meeting of the State Legislature, as there will be there an outside gathering of the very ablest men of that State.

"And the next point, that you should, at the earliest possible day of the session of our own legislature, elect a man as governor, whose name and character will conciliate as well as give confidence to all the men of the State. If we do act, I really think this half the battle; a man upon whose temper the State can rely.

"I say nothing about a convention, as I understand, on all hands, that that is a fixed fact, and I have confined myself to answering your question. I will be much obliged to you if you will write me soon and fully from Columbia. It is impossible to write to you, with the constant interruption of the office, and as you want Cobb's opinions, not mine, I send this to you.   Yours,   W. H. T."

The original of the above letter is in my possession.

¹ Ten years before, this man, then engaged in treasonable schemes, dating his letter at Washington, "House of Representatives, September 2, 1850," wrote to General Quitman, then Governor of Mississippi, on whom the mantle of Calhoun, as chief conspirator against American Nationality, had worthily fallen, saying:—" When the President of the United States commands me to do one act, and the Executive of Mississippi commands me to do another thing, inconsistent with the first order, I obey the Governor of my State. To Mississippi I owe allegiance, and, because she commands me, I owe obedience to the United States."—*Life and Correspondence of John A. Quitman:* by J. F. H. Claiborne, ii. 63. This is the pure doctrine of Supreme State Sovereignty, on which the conspirators founded their justification for the so-called secession of the States from the Union.

* The iniquity of this recommendation of Cobb is made apparent by the fact, that it was a common practice for the planter to receive pay for his crop in advance. The crop now to "go forward" was already paid for. The money to be received, on its delivery, was for the next year's crop, which would never be delivered. Here was a proposition for a scheme to swindle Northern men to the amount of many millions of dollars.

terest so strong in the movement, I fear they will be violent beyond control." The seizure of the Government, before Mr. Lincoln's inauguration, was a part of the plan of operations. "The successful, unrestricted installation of Lincoln," wrote this viper, nestled in the warm bosom of the Republic, "is the beginning of the end of Slavery."[1] Thompson afterward took up arms against the Republic, plotted the blackest crimes against the people of his country while finding an asylum in Canada, and was finally charged with complicity in the murder of President Lincoln. Floyd, indicted for enormous frauds on the Government while in office, perished ignobly, after wearing the insignia of a brigadier-general among the insurgent enemies of his country.

The Governors and Legislatures of several of the Slave-labor States took early action against the National Government. The South Carolina politicians moved first. They were traditionally rebellious, gloried in their turbulence, and were jealous of any leadership or priority of action in the great drama of Treason about to be opened.

Governor Gist called the South Carolina Legislature to meet in extraordinary session, in the old State House at Columbia, on Monday, the 5th of November, for the purpose of choosing, on the following day, Presidential electors.[2] In his message to both Houses, he recommended the authorization of a convention of the people, to consider the expediency of with-

drawing the State from the Union, in the event of Lincoln's election. He expressed a desire that such withdrawal should be accomplished. "The indications from many of the Southern States," he said, "justify the conclusion that the secession of South Carolina will be immediately followed, if not adopted simultaneously, by them, and ultimately by the entire South. . . . The State has, by great unanimity, declared that she has the right peaceably to secede,[3] and no power on earth can rightfully prevent it. If, in the exercise of arbitrary power, and forgetful of the lessons of history, the Government of the United States should attempt coercion, it will become our solemn duty to meet force by force; and, whatever may be the decision of the conven-

THE OLD STATE HOUSE AT COLUMBIA.

---

[1] Letter to Mr. Peterson, of Mississippi. It fell into the hands of United States troops while in that region, in 1863.

[2] In South Carolina, political power had always been as far removed from the people as possible. The Governor of the State and the Presidential electors were, by a provision of the State Constitution, chosen by the Legislature, and not directly by the people.

[3] In 1852, a State Convention in South Carolina reiterated the sentiments of the Nullification Convention twenty years before, and declared that the State had a "right to secede from the Confederacy whenever the occasion should arise justifying her, in her judgment, in taking that step." The Convention informed the world that the State forbore the immediate exercise of that right from considerations of expediency only.

tion representing the sovereignty of the State, and amenable to no earthly tribunal, it shall, during the remainder of my administration, be carried out to the letter, regardless of any hazard that may surround its execution." He recommended the immediate arming, "with the most efficient weapons of modern warfare," every white man in the State between the ages of eighteen and forty-five, and placing the whole military force of the Commonwealth "in a position to be used at the shortest notice, and with the greatest efficiency." He also recommended the immediate acceptance of ten thousand volunteers, to be officered and drilled, and held in readiness to be called upon at the shortest notice.

These recommendations to prepare for revolt were made on the day before the election of Mr. Lincoln. They met with a hearty response. On that evening, prominent South Carolinians, who were in attendance, were serenaded and made speeches. One of these was James Chesnut, Jr., a member of the United States Senate. He told the crowd of listeners that he had no doubt of the election of Mr. Lincoln on the morrow, and that then they had arrived "at the initial point of a new departure. We have two ways before us," he said, "in one of which, whether we will or not, we must tread. . . . In both lie dangers, difficulties, and troubles, which no human foresight can foreshadow or perceive; but they are not equal in magnitude. One is beset with humiliation, dishonor, *émeutes*, rebellions—with submission, in the beginning, to all, and at all times, and confiscation and slavery in the end. The other, it is true, has its difficulties and trials, but no disgrace. Hope, duty, and honor shine along the path." "The Black Republicans," he said, "claim the dogmas of the Declaration of Independence as part of the Constitution, and that it is their right and duty to so administer the Government as to give full effect to them. The people now must choose whether they will be governed by enemies or govern themselves. For myself, I would unfurl the Palmetto flag, fling it to the breeze, and, with the spirit of a brave man, determine to live and die as becomes our glorious ancestry, and ring the clarion notes of defiance in the ears of an insolent foe." He spoke of the undoubted right of South Carolina to withdraw from the Union, and recommended its immediate action in that direction, saying, "the other Southern States will flock to our standard." His speech was received with vehement applause, and met with greetings of satisfaction throughout the State.

In a similar manner, W. W. Boyce, who had been a member of Congress since 1853, responded to a serenade on the following evening,* from the balcony of the Congaree House. "In my opinion," he said, "the South ought not to submit. If you intend to resist, the way to resist in earnest is to act; the way to enact revolution is to stare it in the face. I think the only policy for us is to arm as soon as we receive authentic intelligence of the election of Lincoln. It is for South Carolina, in the quickest manner, and by the most direct means, to withdraw from the Union. Then we will not submit, whether the other Southern States will act with us or with our enemies. . . . When an ancient philosopher wished to inaugurate a revolution, his motto was: To dare! To dare!" From that moment, he was zealously engaged in efforts to destroy his Government.

* November 6, 1860.

From the same balcony Edmund Ruffin, of Virginia, a white-haired old man, made a speech to the excited people. He was well known as a political and agricultural writer, and a warm personal friend and admirer of John C. Calhoun and his principles. He had made it an important part of the business of his life to applaud the system of Slavery, and to create in the Slave-labor States a hatred of the people of the Free-labor States. He soon afterward acquired the unenviable distinction of having raised the first spadefull of earth in the construction of military works for the assault on Fort Sumter, and also of having fired the first shot at that fortification.[1] He had now hastened from his home in Virginia to Columbia, to urge the importance of immediate secession. "I have studied the question now before the country," he said, "for years. It has been the one great idea of my life. The defense of the South, I verily believe, is only to be secured through the lead of South Carolina. Old as I am, I have come here to join her in that

lead. I wish Virginia was as ready as South Carolina, but, unfortunately, she is not. But the first drop of blood spilled on the soil of South Carolina will bring Virginia and every other Southern State to her side."

It had been agreed that revolutionary movements should commence immediately after the fact should be made known that Mr. Lincoln was elected. Accordingly, on the evening of the 7th,* a dispatch went up to Columbia from Charleston, saying that many of the National officers had resigned. That morning, the United States District Court had

* November, 1860.

EDMUND RUFFIN.

assembled in Charleston, over which one of the leaders of rebellion, Judge A. G. Magrath, presided. The Grand Jury, according to instructions, declined to make any presentments. They said that the action of the ballot-box on the previous day had destroyed all hopes of a permanent confederacy of the "Sovereign States," and that the public mind was constrained to "rise above the consideration of details in the administration of law and justice, up to the vast and solemn issues that have been forced upon us—issues which involve the existence of the Government of which this Court is the organ." They therefore declined to act. This solemn judicial farce was perfected by the formal resignation of Judge Magrath. With ludicrous gravity, he said to the jurors:—"For the last time I have, as Judge of the United

---

[1] Ruffin was in Richmond at the close of the following summer, and visited the National prisoners who were captured at the battle of Bull's Run in July. He told them that he was then a resident of Charleston, in South Carolina, and boasted that he was the person who fired the first shot at Sumter. Mr. Ely, member of Congress, who was among the prisoners, speaks of him in his *Journal*, kept while in confinement in Richmond, as "a patriarchal citizen, whose long locks extended over his shoulders, whitened by the snows of more than seventy winters." Ruffin did not appear prominently in the war that ensued. He survived the conflict, in which he lost all of his property. On Saturday, the 17th of June, 1865, he committed suicide by blowing off the top of his head with a gun, at the residence of his son, near Danville, in Virginia. He left a note, in which he said:—"I cannot survive the liberties of my country." The wretched man was then almost eighty years of age.

States, administered the laws of the United States within the limits of South Carolina. So far as I am concerned, the Temple of Justice, raised under the Constitution of the United States, is now closed." He then laid aside his gown, and retired.

A. G. MAGRATH.

The Collector of Customs at Charleston, C. J. Colcock, and James Gonner, the United States District Attorney, resigned at the same time; and B. C. Pressley, the National Sub-treasurer, also announced his determination to resign, as soon as he could with due respect to President Buchanan. Although a convention to make a formal declaration of the withdrawal of the State from the Union had not yet been authorized, the conspirators and their political instruments throughout South Carolina now acted as if disunion had been actually accomplished.

On the morning of the 7th,* when the telegraph had flashed intelligence of Lincoln's election over the length and breadth of the land, and bore tidings of great joy elsewhere because of the auspicious event, the enthusiasm of the rebellious people in Charleston was unbounded and irrepressible. The conspirators and their friends greeted each other with signs of the greatest exultation. They grasped each other's hands, and some of them cordially embraced, in the ecstasy of their pleasure. The Palmetto flag was everywhere unfurled; and from the crowded streets went up cheer after cheer for a Southern Confederacy. All day the enthusiasm was kept up by speeches, harangues, and the booming of cannon; and, at evening, the city was illuminated by bonfires. The wished-for pretext for insurrection was at hand, and the master spirits of treason were everywhere jubilant. Their work, begun so hopefully in the Convention at Charleston, in April, was now well-nigh finished in November.

* November, 1860.

PALMETTO FLAG.

The germ of revolution then planted had expanded, and budded, and blossomed, and now promised abundant fruit.

There was intense excitement at Columbia, on the morning after the election. Governor Gist was the recipient of many messages by telegraph:—"The Governor and Council are in session," said one from Raleigh, North Carolina. "The people are very much excited. North Carolina is ready to secede."—"Large numbers of Bell men," said another, from Montgomery, Alabama, "headed by T. H. Watts,[1] have declared for secession, since the announcement of Lincoln's election. The State will undoubtedly secede." —"The hour for action has come," said a message from Milledgeville, Geor-

---

[1] Thomas H. Watts was a "Bell-Everett" elector, but espoused the cause of the conspirators at the very beginning of their open career. He was elected Governor of Alabama in 1863, and used his official power to its utmost in favor of the rebellion.

gia. "This State is ready to assert her rights and independence. The leading men are eager for the business."—"There is a great deal of excitement here," said a dispatch from Washington City; "several extreme Southern men, in office, have donned the Palmetto cockade,[1] and declared themselves ready to march South."—"If your State secedes," said another, from Richmond, Virginia, "we will send you troops of volunteers to aid you."—"Placards are posted about the city," said a message from New Orleans, "calling a convention of those favorable to the organization of a corps of *Minute-men*. The Governor is all right."—"Be firm," said a second dispatch from Washington; "a large quantity of arms will be shipped South from the Arsenal here, to-morrow. The President is perplexed. His feelings are with the South, but he is afraid to assist them openly."—"The bark *James Gray*, owned by Cushing's Boston line, lying at our wharves," said a message from Charleston, "has hoisted the Palmetto flag, and fired a salute of fifteen guns, under direction of her owner. The *Minute-men* throng the streets with Palmetto cockades in their hats. There is great rejoicing here."

SECESSION COCKADE.

Stimulated by these indications of sympathy, the South Carolina Legislature took bold and vigorous action. Joint resolutions were offered in both Houses, providing for the calling of a State Convention at an early day, for the purpose of formally declaring the withdrawal of the State from the Union. These, generally, contemplated immediate separate State action, before the excitement caused by the election should subside, and the heads of the people should become cool and capable of sober reflection. But there were able men in that Legislature, who foresaw the perils which a single State, cut loose from her moorings during a terrible storm of passion, would have to encounter, and pleaded eloquently for the exercise of reason and prudence. They were as zealous as their colleagues for ultimate secession, but regarded the co-operation of at least the other Cotton-growing States as essential to success. "If the State, in her sovereign capacity, determines that secession will produce the co-operation which we have so earnestly sought," said Mr. McGowan, of Abbeville, "then it shall have my hearty approbation. . . . If South Carolina, in Convention assembled, deliberately secedes—separate and alone, and, without hope of co-operation, decides to cut loose from her moorings, surrounded as she is by Southern sisters in like circumstances—I will be one of her crew, and, in common with every true son of hers, will endeavor, with all the power that God has given me, to

> 'Spread all her canvas to the breeze,
> Set every threadbare sail,
> And give her to the God of storms,
> The lightning and the gale.' "

But these cautious men were overborne by the fiery zealots. One of these (Mullins, from Marion), in his eagerness to hurry the State out of the Union, revealed not only the fact that the heads and hearts of the great mass of the people of South Carolina were not in unison with the desperate

---

[1] Made of blue silk ribbon, with a button in the center, bearing the image of a Palmetto-tree.

politicians who were exciting them to revolt, but another fact, afterward made clear—that months before Mr. Lincoln's election, emissaries of the conspirators had been sent to Europe, to prepare the way for aid and recognition of the contemplated Southern Confederacy by foreign powers. "If we wait for co-operation," he said, "*Slavery and State Rights will be abandoned, State Sovereignty and the cause of the South lost forever;* and we would be subjected to a dominion, the parallel to which is that of the poor Indian under the British East India Company. When we have pledged ourselves to take the State out of the Union, and place it on record, then I am willing to send a commissioner to Georgia, or any other Southern State, to announce our determination, and to submit the question whether they will join us or not. We have it from high authority, that the representative of one of the imperial powers of Europe, in view of the prospective separation of one or more of the Southern States from the present Confederacy, has made propositions in advance for the establishment of such relations between it and the government about to be established in this State, as will insure to that power such a supply of cotton for the future as their increasing demand for that article will require."[1]

Led by Robert Barnwell Rhett, Senior, the extremists in the South Carolina Legislature held sway in that body, and on the 9th of November a bill calling a convention for the purpose of secession passed the Senate, and was concurred in by the House on the 12th. It provided for the election of delegates on the 6th of December, to meet in convention on the 17th of that month. This accomplished, Messrs. Chesnut and Hammond formally offered the resignation of their seats in the Senate of the United States. The offer was accepted with great applause, as the beginning of the dissolution of the Union.

Georgia was the first to follow the bad example of South Carolina. Its Legislature was convened on the 7th of November. Robert Toombs and Alfred Iverson, then United States Senators, and others, had been laboring with intense zeal, during the Presidential canvass, to arouse the people to revolt when the leaders should give the signal. Many influential men were co-workers with them. It was exceedingly difficult to seduce the people of that State from their affection for the Union. They succeeded, however, in producing a general ferment and unrest throughout the State; and, by falsehoods, impassioned addresses, and, in some cases, intimations of impending wrath for Union men, they confused, distracted, and divided the people. Toombs, like Rhett, was anxious for the immediate and separate secession of his State.

By the time the Legislature met, which was on the day after the Presidential election,[*] there had been created quite a strong disunion feeling throughout the State. It permeated the woof of society, *November 7.* and was prominent in the whole social fabric. The Legislature was divided in sentiment; and a majority of them did not coincide with the Speaker, who, in opening the session, declared that the triumph of the Republican party would lead to a nullification of the Fugitive Slave Law; the exclusion of Slavery from the Territories; the non-admission of any more Slave States

---

[1] This matter is elucidated in another portion of this work.

into the Union; the abolition of Slavery in the District of Columbia; the desecration of the Church, by the installation therein of an "Anti-slavery God;" the dissolution of every bond of union between the North and the South, and a practical application of the theory that the Republic could not exist, half slave and half free. These predictions of the Speaker, through the operations of war, were fulfilled to the letter. They are now History.

Governor Joseph E. Brown's message to the Legislature of Georgia was long, temperate in language, but very hostile toward the people of the North. After reviewing, at great length, the legislation in several of the Northern States concerning the Fugitive Slave Law, he urged the enactment, as a retaliatory measure, of a law making it a penal offense to introduce any goods, wares, or merchandise into Georgia from any of those States. "In my opinion," he said, "the time for bold, decided action, has arrived." He was opposed to secession as a remedy for existing evils, and did not like the project of a Southern Convention of States looking to that end, which had been proposed; yet, he recommended the appropriation of a million of dollars for the purpose of arming the State.

The Legislature discussed the exciting topics presented to them with calmness. It was generally agreed that the State could not remain within the Union excepting on certain conditions, such as the repeal of the Personal Liberty Laws existing in some of the Free-labor States, and the enactment of laws by Congress for the protection of Slave property in the Territories. By a heavy majority they voted that a "Sovereign State" of the Union had a right to secede from it, adopting as their own the doctrine put forth by the Governor in his message, that the States of the Union are not subordinate to the National Government; were not created by it, and do not belong to it; that *they* created the National Government; from them it derives its powers; to them it is responsible, and, when it abuses the trust reposed in it, they, as equal sovereigns, have a right to resume the powers respectively delegated to it by them.

This is the sum and substance of the doctrine of State supremacy, as defined and inculcated by Calhoun and his followers, for the evident purpose of weakening the attachment of the people to the Union, and so dwarfing their patriotism that narrow State pride should take the place of the lofty sentiment of nationality, and predispose them to acquiescence in the scheme for forming a "Southern Confederacy," to be composed of the Slave-labor States. That definition of the character of our Government has no real foundation in truth, discoverable in the teachings or actions of the founders of the Republic who framed the National Constitution, nor in the revealments of history.[1] It defines, with proximate accuracy, the char-

---

[1] Let us here consider two or three expressions of those founders:—

"I hold it for a fundamental point, that an individual independence of the States is utterly irreconcilable with the idea of an aggregate sovereignty."—*Letter to Edmund Randolph*, April 8, 1787, by James Madison.

"The Swiss Cantons have scarce any union at all, and have been more than once at war with one another. How, then, are all these evils to be avoided? Only by such a complete sovereignty in the General Government as will turn all the strong principles and passions above mentioned on its side."—*Speech by Alexander Hamilton in the Constitutional Convention*, June 18, 1787.

"A thirst for power, and the bantling—I had like to have said the MONSTER—sovereignty, which have taken such fast hold of the States individually will, when joined by the many whose personal consequence in the line of State politics will, in a manner, be annihilated, form a strong phalanx against it."—*Letter of Washington to John Jay*, March 10, 1787, on proposed changes in the fundamental laws of the land.—*Life of Jay*, i. 259.

See also, *Two Lectures on the Constitution of the United States*, by Francis Lieber, LL. D.

acter of the Government under the old Confederation, which existed for eight or ten years before the National Constitution became the supreme law of the land; but it is clearly erroneous as applied to the Government which was founded on that Constitution in 1789. Instead of the National Government being a creation of the States as States, it is a creation of the *people* of the original thirteen States existing when the present Government was formed, and is the political creator of every State since admitted into the Union, first as a Territory, and then as a State, solely by the exercise of its potential will expressed by the general Congress. Without the consent of Congress, under the provisions of the Constitution, no State can enter the Union.[1] This subject has received the attention due to its importance in another portion of this work. It is introduced here incidentally, to mark the line of difference between Unionists and Secessionists at the beginning of the great struggle—between those who hold that our Republic is a unit or consolidated nation, composed of distinct commonwealths, and those who hold that it is only a league of Sovereign States, whose existence may be ended by the withdrawal, at its own pleasure, of any member of the league. We will only add, that the leaders in the great rebellion found their full justification in the doctrine of the supremacy of the States, which, if it be the true interpretation of our system of government, makes secession and consequent disunion lawful.

Whilst the Georgia Legislature was considering the great questions of the day, and Robert Toombs and other conspirators were urging them to treasonable action, Alexander H. Stephens, a leading man in intellect and personal character in that State, and for a long time its representative in Congress, addressed a large concourse of people,[a] in the Assembly Chamber at Milledgeville. Toombs had harangued them on the previous evening, with his accustomed arrogance of manner and insolence of speech. He denounced the National Government as a curse, and made many false charges concerning its partiality to Northern interests, to the injury of Southern interests. He also urged the Legislature to act on the subject of Secession, independent of the people. He was "afraid of conventions," he said; that is to say, he was afraid to trust the people. His language was violent and seditious in the extreme.[2] He demanded unquestioning acquiescence in his secession schemes, and, with the bravado characteristic of a nature lacking true courage, he said:—"I ask you to give me the sword; for, if you do not give it to me, as God lives, I will take it myself,"—and much more of like tenor. It may not be amiss to say, in this connection, that, during the war that ensued, Toombs was made a brigadier-general in the armies of the conspirators, and, acting in accordance with the maxim, that "Prudence is the better part of valor," was never

* November 14, 1860.

---

[1] See Section 3, Article IV. of the National Constitution.

[2] After telling the people that after the 4th of March ensuing, the National Government, which had from the beginning been controlled by men from the Slave-labor States, would be in the hands of the majority composing the population of the Free-labor States, he said:—" Withdraw your sons from the Army, from the Navy, and every department of the Federal public service. Keep your own taxes in your own coffers. Buy arms with them, and throw the bloody spear into this den of incendiaries and assassins, and let God defend the right. . . . Twenty years of labor, and toils, and taxes, all expended upon preparation, would not make up for the advantage your enemies would gain if the rising sun on the 5th of March should find you in the Union. Then strike while it is yet time!"

known to remain a moment longer than he was compelled to in a place of danger to himself.

Stephens's matter and manner were the reverse of all this. He was calm, cool, dignified, dispassionate, and solemn, but apparently earnest. "My object," he said, "is not to stir up strife, but to allay it; not to appeal to your passions, but to your reason." With the fervor which patriotic impulses inspire, and the apparent candor as well as sagacity of a philosopher, he commented on the election just ended, its significance, and its probable bearing upon the future history of the country, and especially of the Slave-labor States. "Let us reason together," he said. "Shall the people of the South secede from the Union in consequence of the election of Mr. Lincoln to the Presidency of the United States? My countrymen, I tell you frankly, candidly, and earnestly, that I do not think that they ought. In my judgment, the election of no man, constitutionally chosen, to that high office, is sufficient cause for any State to separate from the Union. It ought to stand by and aid still in maintaining the Constitution of the country. To make a point of resistance to the Government, to withdraw from it, because a man has been constitutionally elected, puts us in the wrong. We are pledged to maintain the Constitution. Many of us have sworn to support it. Can we, therefore, for the mere election of a man to the Presidency, and that, too, in accordance with the prescribed forms of the Constitution, make a point of resistance to the Government, by withdrawing from it, without becoming the breakers of that sacred instrument ourselves? Would we not be in the wrong? Whatever fate is to befall this country, let it never be laid to the charge of the people of the South, and especially to the people of Georgia, that we were untrue to our national engagements. Let the fault and the wrong rest upon others. If all our hopes are to be blasted—if the Republic is to go down—let us be found to the last moment standing on the deck, with the Constitution of the United States waving over our heads. Let the fanatics of the North break the Constitution, if that is their fell purpose. Let the responsibility be upon them. I shall speak presently more of their acts; but let not the South—let us not be the ones to commit the aggression. We went into the election with this people. The result was different from what we wished; but the election has been constitutionally held. Were we to make a point of resistance to the Government, and go out of the Union on that account, the record would be made up hereafter against us."

Mr. Stephens then showed, that with a majority of the United States Senate and of the Supreme Court politically opposed to him, the new President would be powerless to do evil to the Slave system. "Why, then," he asked, "should we disrupt the ties of this Union when his hands are tied, and he can do nothing against us?" "My countrymen," he continued, "I am not one of those who believe this Union has been a curse, up to this time. True men, men of integrity, entertain different views from me on this subject. I do not question their right to do so; I would not impugn their motives in so doing. Nor will I undertake to say that this Government of our fathers is perfect. There is nothing perfect in this world, of a human origin—nothing connected with human nature, from man himself to any of his works. . . . But that this Government of our fathers, with all its defects, comes nearer the objects of all good governments than any other on the face of the earth, is my settled conviction. . . . Where will you go, following the sun in its circuit round our globe, to find a government that better protects the liberties of the people, and secures to them the blessings we enjoy? I think that one of the evils that beset us is a surfeit of liberty, an exuberance of priceless blessings for which we are ungrateful."

Mr. Stephens then proceeded to expose the misstatements and dissipate the fallacies uttered by Toombs the previous evening, and was frequently applauded. Toombs was present, and felt the scourge most keenly. With ill-concealed rage and disappointment, he frequently interrupted the speaker, sometimes with tones of anger, and sometimes with those of scorn. These did not disturb the equanimity of his competitor in the least. With perfect coolness, courtesy, and even gentleness, he went forward in his work of apparently endeavoring to stay the rising tide of revolution against the Government he professed to love so well, defending its claim to justice and beneficence. "The great difference between our country and all others, such as France, and England, and Ireland, is," he said, "that here there is popular sovereignty, while there sovereignty is exercised

ROBERT TOOMBS.

by kings and favored classes. This principle of popular sovereignty, however much derided lately, is the foundation of our institutions. Constitutions are but the channels through which the popular will may be expressed. Our Constitution came from the people. They made it, and they alone may rightfully unmake it." . . . "I believe in the power of the people to govern themselves, when wisdom prevails and passion is silent. Look at what has already been done by them for their advancement in all that ennobles man. There is nothing like it in the history of the world. Look abroad from one extent of the country to the other; contemplate our greatness. We are now among the first nations of the earth. Shall it be said, then, that our institutions, founded upon principles of self-government, are a failure? Thus far, our Government is a noble example, worthy of imitation. The gentleman (Mr. Cobb),[1] the other night, said it had proven a failure. A failure in what? In growth? Look at our expanse in national power. Look at our population, and increase in all that makes a people great. A failure? Why, we are the admiration of the civilized world, and present to it the brightest hopes of mankind." With an appropriateness, armed with a peculiar sting for both Toombs and Cobb, and for other demagogues, he added:—"*Some of our public men have failed in their aspirations; that is true, and from that comes a great part of our troubles.*" As soon as prolonged applause ended, Mr. Stephens said:—"No, there is no failure of this Government yet. We have made great advancement under the Constitu-

---

[1] T. R. R. Cobb.

tion, and I cannot but hope that we shall advance higher still. Let us be true to our cause."[1]

Mr. Stephens's speech made a powerful impression throughout the Republic, and many men in the North expressed a wish that Mr. Lincoln might invite him to a seat in his cabinet, as a concession to the South. The true friends of the Government everywhere hoped that it might do its proposed work of allaying the storm of passion, then increasing in violence in the Slave-labor States every hour. That storm had been long gathering. Its elements were marked by intense potency, and it had now burst upon the land with such force that no human work or agency could withstand its blind fury. It was sweeping onward, roaring with the most vehement rage, like a tropical tornado, making every thing bend to its strength. Mr. Stephens himself was lifted by it from the rock of the Constitution, on

. ALEXANDER H. STEPHENS.

which he had so ostentatiously planted his feet at this time, and within ninety days he was riding proudly upon the wings of the tempest, as the second actor in a Confederacy of rebellious men, banded for the avowed purpose of destroying that Constitution, and laying in hopeless ruins the glorious Republic which rested upon it, and which he now professed so ardently to love and admire! He did, indeed, seem to try hard to resist the storm for several weeks; and, during that time, told his countrymen some sober truths concerning the control of the National Government by the Slave interest from its beginning, which should have made the cheeks of every conspirator crimson with shame, because of his mean defiance of every principle of honor and true manhood—his wickedness without excuse.

In the State Convention of Georgia, early in January, 1861, Mr. Stephens said:—"I must declare here, as I have often done before, and which has been repeated by the greatest and wisest of statesmen and patriots in this and other lands, that it is the best and freest Government, the most equal in its rights, the most just in its decisions, the most lenient in its measures, and the most inspiring in its principles to elevate the race of men, that the sun of heaven ever shone upon. Now, for you to attempt to overthrow such a

---

[1] In a private letter, written eleven days after this speech (dated "Crawfordsville, Ga., Nov. 25, 1860 "), Mr. Stephens revealed the fact that in him the patriot was yet subservient to the politician—that his aspirations were really more sectional than national. He avowed that his attachment to Georgia was supreme, and that the chief object of his speech at Milledgeville, on the 14th, was not so much for the preservation of the Union as the security of unity of action in his State. "The great and leading object aimed at by me, in Milledgeville," he said, " was *to produce harmony on a right line of policy*. If the worst comes to the worst, as it may, and our State has to quit the Union, it is of the utmost importance that all our people should be united cordially in this course." After expressing a desire that the rights of Georgia might be secured "in the Union," he said :— " If, after making an effort, we shall fail, then all our people will be united in making or adopting the last resort, the *ultima ratio regum* "—the last argument of kings—the force of arms. He then predicted, that when the Union should be dissevered, "at the North, anarchy will ensue," yet he was doubtful whether the South would be any better off.

Government as this, under which we have lived for more than three-quarters of a century—in which we have gained our wealth, our standing as a nation, our domestic safety, while the elements of peril are around, with peace and tranquillity, accompanied with unbounded prosperity and rights unassailed—is the hight of madness, folly, and wickedness, to which I can neither lend my sanction nor my vote."[1] A month later, he was Vice-President of a Confederacy of traitors to that Government! Indeed, in the first speech here cited he had provided himself with means for escape, should there be an occasion, growing out of a perhaps foreshadowed necessity, by declaring:—
"Should Georgia determine to go out of the Union, I speak for one, though my views might not agree with them, whatever the result may be, I shall bow to the will of the people of my State.[2] Their cause is my cause, and their destiny is my destiny; and I trust this will be the ultimate course of

---

[1] In this speech, Mr. Stephens said, truly, that the Slave-labor States had always received from the National Government all they had ever asked. When they demanded it, the Slave-trade was allowed, by a special provision in the Constitution, for twenty years. When they asked for a three-fifths representation in Congress for their slaves, it was granted. When they asked for the return of fugitive slaves, a provision of the Constitution and special laws were made for that purpose. When they asked for more territory, they received Louisiana, Florida, and Texas. "We have always had the control of the General Government," he said, "and can yet, if we remain in it, and are as united as we have been. We have had a majority of the Presidents chosen from the South, as well as the control and management of most of those chosen from the North. We have had sixty years of Southern Presidents to their twenty-four, thus controlling the Executive Department. So of the Judges of the Supreme Court; there have been eighteen from the South, and but eleven from the North. Although nearly four-fifths of the judicial business has arisen in the Free States, yet a majority of the Court has always been from the South. This we have received, *so as to guard against any interpretation unfavorable to us.* In like manner we have been equally watchful to guard our interests in the Legislative branch of the Government. In choosing the Presidents of the Senate, *pro tempore,* we have had twenty-four to their eleven. Speakers of the House, we have had twenty-three and they twelve. While the majority of the Representatives, from their greater population, have always been from the North, yet we have generally secured the Speaker, because he, to a great extent, shapes and controls the legislation of the country. Nor have we had any less control in every other department of the General Government. Attorney-generals we have had fourteen, while the North have had but five. Foreign Ministers we have had eighty-six, and they but fifty-four." He then went on to show that while three-fourths of the business demanding diplomatic agents abroad was from the Free-labor States, his section had had the principal Embassies; that a vast majority of higher officers of the Army and Navy were from the South, while a larger portion of the soldiers and sailors were drawn from the North; and that two-thirds of the clerks in the Departments at Washington had been taken from the Slave-labor States, while they had only about one-third of the white population. During the same time, over three-fourths of the revenue collected for the support of the Government was uniformly raised from the North. ... The expense for the transportation of the mails in the Free-labor States was, by the Report of the Postmaster-general for 1860, a little over $13,000,000, while the income was $19,000,000. But in the Slave-labor States, the cost of the transportation of the mails was $14,716,000, while the revenue from the same was $8,001,026; leaving a deficit of $6,704,974.

In view of all this, Mr. Stephens might well ask, as he did, "For what purpose will you break up this Union—this American Government, established by our common ancestry, cemented and built up by their sweat and blood, and founded on the broad principles of *Right, Justice,* and *Humanity?*"

[2] In contrast with this subserviency to the idea of State supremacy, and with more enlarged views of the duty of American citizens, Henry Clay, as much interested in Slavery as Mr. Stephens, once said on the floor of Congress, in rebuke of disunion sentiments:—" If Kentucky, to-morrow, unfurls the banner of resistance, I never will fight under that banner; I owe a *paramount* allegiance to the whole Union—a subordinate one to my own State." A writer in the New York *Evening Post* ("W. L. P."), of February 6th, 1865, in a long poem, called "Aleck and Abe," thus alludes to Stephens's defection, which some have attributed to "coercion:"

"But by and by, our doleful friend
  Received a rousing start,
As Yancey waved his lucifers
  To ' fire the Southern heart.'
' Hold, there !' shrieked Aleck, in dismay;
  ' Was ever wretch so rash ?
If you ignite that magazine,
  You'll blow us all to smash !'
Outspoke the Fire-fiend of the South:
  ' Not so, by grandest odds—
If I let off this magazine
  We all become as gods !'
' You lie,' cried Aleck, ' in your throat;
  And more, you *know* you lie !'

Screamed Yancey, ' You shall eat those words,
  As sure as I am I.'
And, sooth, he did it in a twink,
  With many a wry grimace ;
As Jeff. and Toombs stood by, and shook
  A halter in his face.
And when the words were all devoured,
  With right hand on his breast,
He whimpered, ' Pray, forgive me, friends;
  Indeed, I did but jest.
And now I've had my little joke,
  And you your natural "swear;"
I'm all agog to back your aims—
  What's first to do or dare !' "

all. Let us call a convention of the people; let all these matters be submitted to it; and when the will of a majority of the people has thus been expressed, the whole State will present one unanimous voice in favor of whatever may be demanded."

Influences more powerful than any Mr. Stephens could command were at work upon the public mind. Only two days before his speech ^November 12, was pronounced, a Military Convention was held at Milledge- 1860. ville,[a] which was addressed by the Governor of the State, in very incendiary language. He affirmed the *right* of secession, and also the duty of all the Southern States to sustain the action of the South Carolina Legis- lature. "I would like," he said "to see Federal troops dare attempt the coercion of a seceding Southern State. For every Georgian who should fall in a conflict thus incited, the lives of two Federal soldiers should expiate the outrage on State Sovereignty." These were brave words in the absence of all danger. When that danger was nigh—when "Federal sol- ^November, diers" under Sherman, just four years later,[b] were marching 1864. through Georgia, in triumphant vindication of the National au-

OSEPH E. BROWN.

thority, Governor Brown and many mem- bers of the Legislature were trembling fugi- tives from that very capitol where Toombs, and Cobb, and Iverson, and Benning, and Brown himself, had fulminated their foolish threats.

The Military Convention, by a heavy majority, voted in favor of secession; and this action had great weight with the Legislature and the people. On ^November 13. the following day,[c] the Legis- lature voted an appropriation of a million of dollars for arming and equipping the militia of the State; and on the 7th of December, an act, calling a convention of

^1861. the people, was passed, which provided for the election of dele- gates on the 2d of January,[d] and their assemblage on the 16th. The preamble to the bill declared that, in the judgment of that Assembly, the "present crisis in National affairs demands resistance," and that "it is the privilege of the people to determine the mode, measure, and time of such resistance." Power to do this was given to the Convention by the act.

On the 14th of December, a large meeting of the members of the Legis- lature assembled in the Senate Chamber, and agreed to an address to the people of South Carolina, Alabama, Mississippi, and Florida, urging upon them the importance of co-operation, rather than separate State action, in the matter of secession. "Our people must be united," they said; "our common interests must be preserved." The address was signed by fifty-two members of the Legislature. It was so offensive to the Hotspurs of the South Carolina State Convention, that that body refused to receive it. We shall again refer to the action of the Georgia Legislature.

The Legislature of Mississippi assembled at Jackson early in November, and adjourned on the 30th. The special object of the session was to make preparations for the secession of the State. An act was passed, providing for a Convention, to be held on the 7th of January; and the 20th of December was the day appointed by it for the election of delegates thereto. The Governor (John J. Pettus) was authorized to appoint commissioners to visit each of the Slave-labor States, for the purpose of officially informing the governors or legislatures thereof, that the State of Mississippi had called a Convention, "to consider the present threatening relations of the Northern and Southern sections of the Confederacy, aggravated by the recent election of a President upon principles of hostility to the States of the South; and to express the earnest hope of Mississippi, that those States will co-operate with her in the adoption of efficient measures for their common defense and safety." A portion of the Legislature was for immediate separation and secession. The press of the State was divided in sentiment, and so were the people, while their representatives in Congress were active traitors to their government. One of these (Lucius Quintius Curtius Lamar, a native of Georgia, who remained in Congress until the 12th of January, 1861, and was afterward sent to the Russian Court, as a diplomatic agent of the conspirators), submitted to the people of Mississippi, before the close of November, 1860, a plan for a "Southern Confederacy." After reciting the ordinance by which Mississippi was created a State of the Union, and proposing her formal withdrawal therefrom, the plan proposed that the

LUCIUS Q. C. LAMAR.

State of Mississippi should "consent to form a Federal Union" with all the Slave-labor States, the Territory of New Mexico, and the Indian Territory west of Arkansas, "under the name and style of the United States of America, and according to the tenor and effect of the Constitution of the United States," with slight exceptions. It proposed to continue in force all laws and treaties of the United States, so far as they applied to Mississippi, until the new Confederation should be organized, and that all regulations, contracts, and engagements made by the old Government should remain in force. It provided that the Governor of Mississippi should perform the functions of President of the new United States, within the limits of that State, and that all public officers should remain in place until the new government should be established. It was also provided that the accession of nine States should give effect to the proposed ordinance of confederation; and that, when such accession should occur, it should be the duty of the Governor to order an election of Congressmen and Presidential Electors. This scheme, like a score of others put forth by disloyal men, ambitious to appear in history as the founders of a new empire, soon found its appropriate place in the tomb of forgotten things.

The southern portion of Alabama was strongly in favor of secession, while the northern portion was as strongly in favor of Union. The Governor (Andrew B. Moore) sympathized with the secessionists, and, with Yancey and others, stirred up the people to revolt. He had been active in procuring the passage of joint resolutions by the Legislature of that State, ^{a February 24, 1860} long before the Presidential election,[a] which provided, in the event of the election of the Republican candidate, for a convention to consider what should be done ; in other words, to declare the secession of the State from the Union, in accordance with the long and well-devised plan of the conspirators. So early as October, Herschell V. Johnston, the candidate for Vice-President on the Douglas ticket, ^{b October 24.} declared, in a speech in the Cooper Institute, New York,[b] that Alabama was ripe for revolt, in the event of Mr. Lincoln's election—"pledged," he said, "to withdraw from the Union, and has appropriated two hundred thousand dollars for military contingencies."[1] In an address to the people of the State, early in November, the Governor declared that, in his opinion, "the only hope and future security for Alabama and other Slaveholding States, is in secession from the Union." On the 6th of December he issued a proclamation, assuring the people that the contingency contemplated by the Legislature had occurred, namely the election of Mr. Lincoln, and, by the authority given him by that body, he ordered delegates to be chosen on the 24th of December, to meet in convention on ^{c 1861.} the 7th of January.[c] Five days before that election, the Alabama Conference of the "Methodist Church South," a very large and most influential body, sitting at Montgomery, resolved that they believed "African Slavery, as it existed in the Southern States of the Republic, to be a wise, humane, and righteous institution, approved of God, and calculated to promote, to the highest possible degree, the welfare of the slave ;[2] that the election of a sectional President of the United States was evidence of the hostility of the majority to the people of 'the South,' and which, in fact, if not in form, dissolves the compact of Union between the States, and drives the aggrieved party to assert their independence ;" and therefore they said, "our hearts are with the South, and should they ever need our hands to assist in achieving our independence, we shall not be found wanting in the hour of danger."[3]

Florida, the most dependent upon the Union for its prosperity of all the States, and the recipient of most generous favors from the National Government, was, by the action of its treasonable politicians, and especially by its representatives in Congress, made the theater of some of the earliest and most active measures for the destruction of the Republic. Its Legislature met at Tallahassee on the 26th of November, and its Governor, Madison S. Perry, in his message at the opening of the session, declared that the

---

¹ Report of Johnson's speech, in the New York *World*, October 25, 1860.

² See Note 3, page 88.

³ In the first act of the melodrama of the rebellion, there were some broad farces. One of these is seen in the action of the Grand Jury of the United States for the Middle District of Alabama. That body made the following presentment at the December Term, 1860:—

"That the several States of Massachusetts, New Hampshire, Vermont, New York, Ohio, and others, have nullified, by acts of their several Legislatures, several laws enacted by the Congress of the Confederation for the protection of persons and property ; and that for many years said States have occupied an attitude of hostility to the interests of the people of the said Middle District of Alabama. And the said Federal Government, having failed to execute its enactments for the protection of the property and interests of said Middle District, and this court having no jurisdiction in the premises, this Grand Jury do present the said Government as worthless, impotent, and a *nuisance*.   C. G. GUNTHER, *Foreman*,
                                                                            and nineteen others."

"domestic peace and future prosperity" of the State depended upon "secession from their faithless and perjured confederates." He alluded to the argument of some, that no action should be taken until they knew whether the policy of the new Administration would be hostile to their interests or not; and, with the gravity of the most earnest disciple of Calhoun, he flippantly said:—"My countrymen, if we wait for an overt act of the Federal Government, our fate will be that of the white inhabitants of St. Domingo. Why wait?" he asked. "What is this Government? It is but the trustee, the common agent of all the States, appointed by them to manage their affairs, according to a written constitution, or power of attorney. Should the Sovereign States then—the principals and the partners in the association —for a moment tolerate the idea that their action must be graduated by the will of their agent? The idea is preposterous." This was but another mode of expressing the doctrine of State Supremacy.

Louisiana was rather slow to move in the direction of treason. Her worst enemy, John Slidell, then misrepresenting her in the Senate of the United States, had been engaged for years in corrupting the patriotism of her sons, and had been aided in his task by Judah P. Benjamin, a Hebrew unworthy of his race, and others of less note. Slidell was universally detested by right-minded men for his political dishonesty,[1] his unholy ambition, his lust for aristocratic rank and power, and his enmity to republican institutions. He had tried in vain, during the summer and autumn of 1860, to engage many of the leading men in Louisiana in treasonable schemes. With others, such as Thomas O. Moore (the Governor of the State), and a few men in authority, he was more successful. Among the leading newspapers of the State, the New Orleans *Delta* was the only open advocate of hostility and resistance to the National Government, after the Presidential election.

Governor Moore called an extraordinary session of the Legislature, to meet at Baton Rouge on the 10th of December, giving as a reason the election of Mr. Lincoln by a party hostile to "the people and institutions of the South." In his message he said, he did not think it comported "with the honor and self-respect of Louisiana, as a Slaveholding State, to live under the government of a Black Republican President," although he did not dispute the fact that he had been elected by due form of law. "The question," he said, "rises high above ordinary political considerations. It involves our present honor, and our future existence as a free and independent people." He asserted the right of a State to secede; and hoped that, if any attempt should be made by the National authority "to coerce a Sovereign State, and compel her to submission to an authority she had ceased to recognize," Louisiana would "assist her sister States with the same alacrity and courage that the Colonies assisted each other in their struggle against the despotism of the Old

---

[1] A single incident in the political career of Slidell illustrates not only the dishonesty of his character, but the facilities which are frequently offered for politicians to cheat the people. Slidell had resolved to become a member of Congress. He was rich, but was, personally, too unpopular to expect votes enough to elect him. He resorted to fraud. None but freeholders might vote in Louisiana. Slidell bought, at Government price (one dollar and twenty-five cents an acre), one hundred and eighty-eight acres of land, and deeded it, in small parcels, to four thousand eight hundred and eight of the most degraded population of New Orleans. They went to his district (Plaquemine), where their land lay, and, in a body, gave him their votes for Congress, and elected him! That was in 1842.

World. If I am not mistaken in public opinion," he said, "the Convention, if assembled, will decide that Louisiana will not submit to the Presidency of Mr. Lincoln." The Legislature passed an act providing for a State Convention, to assemble on the 22d of January; and another, appropriating five hundred thousand dollars for military purposes. They listened to a commissioner from Mississippi (Wirt Adams), but refused to authorize the Governor to appoint like agents to visit the Slave-labor States. They gave him authority to correspond with the governors of those States upon the great topic of the day, and adjourned on the 13th, to meet again on the 23d of January.⁴

« 1861.

Texas, under the leadership of its venerable Governor, Samuel Houston, and the influence of a strong Union feeling, held back, when invited by conspirators to plunge into secession. So did Arkansas, Missouri, Kentucky, Tennessee, Virginia, Maryland, and Delaware, all Slave-labor States. The Governor of Tennessee, Isham G. Harris, who was a traitor at heart, and had corresponded extensively with the disunionists of the Cotton-growing States, made great but unsuccessful exertions to link the fortunes of his State with those of South Carolina in the secession movement.

North Carolina took early but cautious action. The most open and influential secessionists in that State were Thomas L. Clingman, then a member of the United States Senate, and John W. Ellis, the Governor of the Commonwealth. They made great efforts to arouse the people of the State to revolt, but failed. The Union sentiment, and the respect for law and the principles of republican government were so deeply implanted in the nature and the habits of the people, that they could not be easily seduced from their allegiance to the National Government. The Legislature met on the 19th of November. An act was passed providing for a Convention, but directing that "no ordinance of said Convention, dissolving the connection of the State of North Carolina with the Federal Government, or connecting it with any other, shall have any force or validity until it shall have been submitted to and ratified by a majority of the qualified voters of the State for members of the General Assembly, to whom it shall be submitted for their approval or rejection;" and that it should be "advertised for at least thirty days in the newspapers of the State, before the people should be called upon to vote on the same."

Such is a brief outline of the preparations for the marshaling of the cohorts of rebellion in the Slave-labor States; for a vigorous assault, not only upon the Republic, but upon the advancing civilization of the age, and the rights of man—upon the cherished institutions of good and free government inherited from the patriots of the old War for Independence, and the hopes of aspirants for freedom throughout the world.

It is evident, in even this shadowy picture, which reveals similarity of expressions and actions in the movements of the opponents of the Government in widely separated portions of the Slave-labor States, that there had been long and thorough preparation for the revolt. This will become more manifest as we proceed in our inquiry; and when, at the close of this work, we shall consider the history of political parties at the beginning of our national career, and the gradual development of radical differences of social and political opinions in sections of the Republic remote from each other, we shall perceive that rebellion and civil war were logical results of the increasing activity of potential antagonisms, controlled and energized by selfish men for selfish purposes.[1]

---

[1] The contemplation of disunion, as an emollient for irritated State pride, had been a habit of thought in Virginia and the more Southern Slave-labor States from the beginning of the Government. Whenever the imperious will of a certain class of politicians in those States was offended by a public policy opposed to its wishes, they were in the habit of speaking of the dissolution of the Union as their remedy for the provocation. They threatened to dissolve the Union in 1795, if Jay's Treaty with Great Britain should be ratified by the United States Senate; and the famous Kentucky and Virginia Resolutions of 1798, in which the doctrine of State Supremacy was broadly inculcated, familiarized the popular mind with the idea that the National Government was only the agent of the States, and might be dismissed by them at any time.

The more concrete and perfect form of these sentiments, embodied in deliberate intentions, was exhibited by John C. Calhoun, as we have observed (note 2, page 41), in 1812. Disloyalty was strongly manifested during the discussions of the Slavery question before the adoption of the Missouri Compromise, in 1820. After the Tariff Act, so obnoxious to the Cotton-growers, became a law, in 1828, the dissolution of the Union was loudly talked of by the politicians of the Calhoun school. "The memorable scenes of our Revolution have again to be acted over," said the *Milledgeville* (Georgia) *Journal;* and the citizens of St. John's Parish, in South Carolina, said, in Convention:—" We have sworn that Congress shall, at our demand, repeal the tariff. If she does not, our State Legislature will dissolve our connection with the Union, and we will take our stand among the nations; and it behooves every true Carolinian ' to stand by his arms,' and to keep the balls of our Legislature pure from foreign intruders."

When, in the autumn of 1832, the famous Nullification Ordinance was passed by the South Carolina Convention, so certain were the mad politicians that composed it of positive success, that they caused a medal to be struck with this inscription:—"JOHN C. CALHOUN, FIRST PRESIDENT OF THE SOUTHERN CONFEDERACY!" Their wicked scheme failed, and Calhoun and his followers went deliberately at work to excite the bitterest sectional strife, by the publication, in the name of Duff Green, as editor and proprietor, of the *United States Telegraph*, at Washington City. At about the same time (1836), a novel was written by Beverly Tucker, of Virginia, called *The Partisan Leader*, in which the doctrine of State Supremacy and the most insidious sectionalism were inculcated in the seductive form of a tale, calculated, as it was intended, to corrupt the patriotism of the Southern people, and prepare them for revolution. This was printed by Duff Green, the manager of Calhoun's organ, and widely circulated in the South.

Finally, "Southern Rights Associations" were formed, having for their object the dissolution of the Union. Concerning this movement, Muscoe R. H. Garnett, who was a Member of Congress from Virginia when the late civil war broke out, wrote to Wm. H. Trescot (afterward Assistant Secretary of State under Mr. Buchanan), in May, 1851, when great preparations were made by the oligarchy for a revolt, saying:—" I would be especially glad to be in Charleston next week, and witness your Convention of delegates from the Southern Rights Associations. The condition of things in your State deeply interests me; her wise foresight and manly independence have placed her at the head of the South, to whom alone true-hearted men can look with any hope or pleasure. Momentous are the consequences which depend upon your action." Garnett mourned over the action of Virginia, in hesitating to go with the revolution. "I do not believe," he said, "that the course of the Legislature is a fair expression of the popular feeling. In the east, at least, the great majority believe in the right of secession, and feel the deepest sympathy with Carolina in opposition to measures which they regard as she does. But the west—Western Virginia—here is the rub! *Only sixty thousand slaves to four hundred and ninety-four thousand whites!* When I consider this fact, and the kind of argument which we have heard in this body, I cannot but regard with the greatest fear the question, whether Virginia would assist Carolina in such an issue. I must acknowledge, my dear Sir, that I look to the future with almost as much apprehension as hope. *You will object to the term Democrat. Democracy, in its original philosophical sense, is indeed incompatible with Slavery, and the whole system of Southern society.* Yet, if we look back, what change will you find made in any of our State Constitutions, or in our legislation, in its general course, for the last fifty years, which was not in the direction of Democracy? Do not its principles and theories become daily more fixed in our practice?—I had almost said, in the opinions of our people, did I not remember with pleasure the great improvement of opinion in regard to the abstract question of Slavery. And if such is the case, what have we to hope for the future? I do not hesitate to say, that if the question is raised between Carolina and the Federal Government, and the latter prevails, the last hope of Republican Government, and, I fear, of Southern civilization, is gone. Russia will then be a better Government than ours."

See pages 92 and 93 of this volume.

CHAPTER III.

ASSEMBLING OF CONGRESS.—THE PRESIDENTS MESSAGE.

HILST the Cotton-growing States were in a blaze of excitement, and the Slave-labor States north of them were surging, and almost insurgent, with conflicting opinions and perplexing doubts and fears, and the Free-labor States were looking on in amazement at the madness of their colleagues, who were preparing to resist the power of the Constitution and laws of the land, the Thirty-Sixth Congress assembled at Washington City. It began its second and last session at the Capitol, on Monday, the 3d of December, 1860. It was on a bright and beautiful morning; and as the eye looked out from the western front of the Capitol upon the city below, the winding Potomac and the misty hights of Arlington beyond, it beheld a picture of repose, strongly contrasting with the spirits of men then assembling in the halls of Congress.

Never, since the birth of the Nation—more than seventy years before—had the people looked with more solemn interest upon the assembling of the National Legislature than at this time. The hoarse cry of Disunion, which had so often been used in and out of Congress by the representatives of the Slave interest, as a bugbear to frighten men of the Free-labor States into compliance with their demands, now had deep significance. Its tone was terribly earnest and defiant, and action was everywhere seen in support of words. It was evident that a crisis in the history of the Republic was present, with demands for forbearance, patience, wisdom, and sound states-

JOHN C. BRECKINRIDGE.

manship, in an eminent degree, to save the nation from dreadful calamities, if not from absolute ruin. Therefore with the deepest anxiety the people, in all parts of the Republic, listened to hear the voice of the President in his Annual Message to Congress, which, it was supposed, would indicate, with clearness and precision, the line of policy which the Government intended to pursue.

Both Houses of Congress convened at noon on the 3d of December. The Senate, with Mr. Breckinridge, the Vice-President, in the chair, was opened by a prayer by the Rev. P. D. Gurley, D. D., the Chaplain of that House, who fervently prayed that all the rulers and the people might be delivered from " erroneous judgments, from misleading influences, and from the sway of evil passions." The House of Representa-